T0028716

EVERYMAN,
I WILL GO WITH THEE
AND BE THY GUIDE,
IN THY MOST NEED
TO GO BY THY SIDE

EVERYMAN'S LIBRARY
POCKET POETS

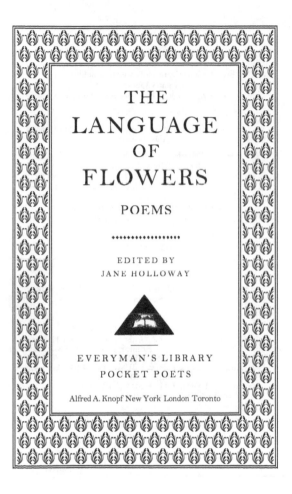

THE
LANGUAGE
OF
FLOWERS

POEMS

••••••••••••••••••

EDITED BY
JANE HOLLOWAY

EVERYMAN'S LIBRARY
POCKET POETS

Alfred A. Knopf   New York   London   Toronto

THIS IS A BORZOI BOOK

PUBLISHED BY ALFRED A. KNOPF

This selection by Jane Holloway first published in
Everyman's Library, 2017
Copyright © 2017 by Everyman's Library

Fourth printing (US)

A list of acknowledgments to copyright owners appears at the back
of this volume.

www.randomhouse.com/everymans
www.everymanslibrary.co.uk

ISBN 978-1-101-90795-5 (US)
978-1-84159-807-9 (UK)

A CIP catalogue record for this book is available from the
British Library

Library of Congress Cataloging-in-Publication Data

Names: Holloway, Jane (Pamela Jane), editor.
Title: The language of flowers: poems / edited by Jane Holloway.
Description: New York: Everyman's Library, 2017. | Series: Pocket poets
Identifiers: LCCN 2017022366 | ISBN 9781101907955 (hardback)
Subjects: LCSH: Flowers–Poetry. | BISAC: POETRY/Anthologies
(multiple authors).
Classification: LCC PN6110.F6 L36 2017 | DDC 808.81/9364213–dc23
LC record available at https://lccn.loc.gov/2017022366

Typography by Peter B. Willberg

Typeset in the UK by Input Data Services Ltd, Isle Abbotts, Somerset

Printed and bound in Germany by GGP Media GmbH, Pössneck

CONTENTS

7

13

FOREWORD

The whole point of the language of flowers being that flowers speak for themselves, the poems in this anthology (itself, of course, meaning a collection of flowers) should do the same. A word, then, about the arrangement only. Since roses and lilies have been made to say a great deal over the centuries, they have demanded a section of their own; otherwise flowers appear as they would in the course of a year. Inevitably this has thrown up problems and colleagues have already disputed some of the decisions made! For greater variety I have interspersed poems from Eastern cultures, rich in floral symbolism and, amongst those from the West, poems from languages other than English. In a final section poets comment either directly or indirectly on the language of flowers, both generally and more specifically as it was understood in the nineteenth century as a secret language of lovers, with origins romantically traced to the harems of Ottoman Turkey. The floral vocabularies which had developed were by then quite elaborate; the glossary at the back gives a flavour. The selection was not easy to make from the wealth of available material; I hope readers will find it enjoyable.

JANE HOLLOWAY
Everyman's Library

From THE HOMERIC HYMN TO DEMETER
PLUTO'S ABDUCTION OF PERSEPHONE

I begin to sing of rich-haired Demeter, awful goddess – of her and her trim-ankled daughter whom Aïdoneus rapt away, given to him by all-seeing Zeus the loud-thunderer.

Apart from Demeter, lady of the golden sword and glorious fruits, she was playing with the deep-bosomed daughters of Oceanus and gathering flowers over a soft meadow, roses and crocuses and beautiful violets, irises also and hyacinths and the narcissus, which Earth made to grow at the will of Zeus and to please the Host of Many, to be a snare for the bloom-like girl – a marvellous, radiant flower. It was a thing of awe whether for deathless gods or mortal men to see: from its root grew a hundred blooms and it smelled most sweetly, so that all wide heaven above and the whole earth and the sea's salt swell laughed for joy. And the girl was amazed and reached out with both hands to take the lovely toy; but the wide-pathed earth yawned there in the plain of Nysa, and the lord, Host of Many, with his immortal horses sprang out upon her – the Son of Cronos, He who has many names.

He caught her up reluctant on his golden car and bare her away lamenting. Then she cried out shrilly with her voice, calling upon her father, the Son of Cronos, who is

most high and excellent. But no one, either of the deathless
gods or of mortal men, heard her voice . . .

Bitter pain seized the heart of Demeter, and she rent the
covering upon her divine hair with her dear hands: her dark
cloak she cast down from both her shoulders and sped, like a
wild-bird, over the firm land and yielding sea, seeking her
child. But no one would tell her the truth, neither god nor
mortal man . . .

      TR. HUGH G. EVELYN-WHITE

SPRING

Hark, hark, the lark at heaven's gate sings,
    And Phoebus gins arise,
His steeds to water at those springs
    On chaliced flowers that lies;
And winking Mary-buds begin
    To ope their golden eyes.
With every thing that pretty is,
    My lady sweet, arise,
        Arise, arise!

WILLIAM SHAKESPEARE
CYMBELINE

'THE FEET OF PEOPLE WALKING HOME'

The feet of people walking home
In gayer sandals go,
The Crocus, till she rises,
The Vassal of the Snow —
The lips at Hallelujah!
Long years of practice bore,
Till bye and bye these Bargemen
Walked singing on the shore.

Pearls are the Diver's farthings
Extorted from the Sea,
Pinions the Seraph's wagon,
Pedestrians once, as we —
Night is the morning's canvas,
Larceny, legacy,
Death but our rapt attention
To immortality.

My figures fail to tell me
How far the village lies,
Whose Peasants are the angels,
Whose Cantons dot the skies,
My Classics veil their faces,
My Faith that dark adores,
Which from its solemn Abbeys
Such resurrection pours!

EMILY DICKINSON (1830–86)   21

'I ASKED THE YELLOW CROCUSES'

I asked the yellow crocuses:
'Where do you spend the winter?'
'Dervish, what are you asking us?
We spend the winter underground.'

I asked the yellow crocuses:
'What do you live on underground?'
'Dervish, what are you asking us?
We live on bits of the mighty power.'

I asked the yellow crocuses:
'Why are your faces so pale?'
'Dervish, what are you asking us?
We draw on the fear of God.'

I asked the yellow crocuses:
'Have you father and mother?'
'Dervish, what are you asking us?
The earth's our mother, the rain's our father.'

I asked the yellow crocuses ...
Staffs in their little hands,
Scriptures on the tip of their tongues,
The crocuses are one with the dervishes.

Pir Sultan is with the dervish brothers,
Face full of holy light,
With the white-bearded forefathers,
The crocuses are one with the dervishes.

22   PIR SULTAN ABDAL (1480–1550)
     TR. RICHARD McKANE

ITALIAN CROCUSES
From *The Lost Girl*

She came upon a bankside all wide with lavender cro-
cuses. The sun was on them for the moment, and they
were opened flat, great five-pointed, seven-pointed
lilac stars, with burning centres, burning with a
strange lavender flame, as she had seen some metal
burn lilac-flamed in the laboratory of the hospital at
Islington. All down the oak-dry bankside they burned
their great exposed stars. And she felt like going
down on her knees and bending her forehead to the
earth in an oriental submission, they were so royal, so
lovely, so supreme. She came again to them in the
morning, when the sky was grey, and they were
closed, sharp clubs, wonderfully fragile on their stems
of sap, among leaves and old grass and wild peri-
winkle. They had wonderful dark stripes running up
their cheeks, the crocuses, like the clear proud stripes
on a badger's face, or on some proud cat. She took a
handful of the sappy, shut, striped flames. In her room
they opened into a grand bowl of lilac fire.

'... FRANKLY I WISH THAT I WERE DEAD'

... frankly I wish that I were dead:
she was weeping as she took her leave from me

and many times she told me this:
'Oh what sadness we have suffered,
Sappho, for I'm leaving you against my will.'

So I gave this answer to her:
'Go, be happy but remember
me there, for you know how we have cherished you,

if not, then I would remind you
[of the joy we have known,] of all
the loveliness that we have shared together;

for many wreaths of violets,
of roses and of crocuses
... you wove around yourself by my side

... and many twisted garlands
which you had woven from the blooms
of flowers, you placed around your slender neck

... and you were anointed with
a perfume, scented with blossom,
... although it was fit for a queen

and on a bed, soft and tender
... you satisfied your desire ...'

24 SAPPHO (B. c. LATE 7TH CENTURY BC)
   TR. JOSEPHINE BALMER

HOW VIOLETS CAME BLUE

Love on a day, wise poets tell,
    Some time in wrangling spent,
Whether the violets should excel,
    Or she, in sweetest scent.

But Venus having lost the day,
    Poor girls, she fell on you:
And beat ye so, as some dare say,
    Her blows did make ye blue.

ROBERT HERRICK (1591–1674)

TO THE VIOLET

Hail to the violet! Sweet careless spread
    Neath each warm bush and covert budding hedge,
In many a pleasing walk have I been led
    To seek thee – promise of spring's earliest pledge –
In modest coyness hanging down its head,
    Unconscious hiding beauties from the eye
And sweetly brooding o'er its graceful form,
    Shunning each vulgar gaze that saunters by
And tim'ly stooping from an April storm;
    As virtue startled by approaching harm
Shrinks from delusion's false betraying hand

With bashful look that more the bosom warms,
So sweetest blossom the coy violet stands
    Tempting the plunderer with a double charm.

JOHN CLARE (1793–1864)

VIOLET

Recently fallen, still with wings out,
she spoke her name to summon us to her darkness.

Not wanting to be seen, but not uncurious,
she spoke her name and let her purple deep eye-pupil
        be peered into.

'Violet,' she said
and showed her heart under its leaf.

Then she leant a little frightened forwards
and picked a hand to pick her.

And her horrified mouseface, sniffed and lifted close,
let its gloom be taken and all the sugar licked off its
        strangeness

while we all stood there saying, 'Violet! Violet!'
fingering her blue bruised skin.

Finally she mentioned
the name of her name

which was something so pin-sharp,
in such a last gasp of a previously unknown language,

it could only be spoken as a scent,
it could only be heard as our amazement.

ALICE OSWALD (1966–)

From THE VIRGIN

THE VIOLET

In Heaven the humble Angels God beheld;
And on the earth, with Angels paralel'd,
The lowlie Virgin view'd. Her modest eye,
Submissive count'nance, thought that did relye
On him that would exalt an humble wight
And make his Mother Alma, ne're in sight,
With vertues, fragrant odours, round beset,
Close to the earth lay like the Violet;
Which, shrowded with its leaves, in covert lyes,
Found sooner by the sent then by the eyes.
    Such was the Virgin rays'd to be Heaven's Queene,
Who on the earth, neglected, was not seene.

HENRY HAWKINS (1571?–1646)

SONNET XCIV

O lovely violet, you were born there
Where my desire of love first came to life.
Beautiful, sad tears were your only waters
That nourished you and often did you bathe.

My lady's love did mercy nourish there
Where the plant lay in that most sacred earth.
Her lovely hand plucked you and then was pleased
To make mine happy with so dear a gift.

That you to flee did want it seemed to me
To that most lovely hand, so I hold you
Against my bare breast tenderly and tight.

Grief and desire my poor bare breast does hold
In my heart's stead, for my poor heart scorns me
And there remains whence you just came, O violet.

LORENZO DE' MEDICI (*c.* 1449–92)
TR. GUIDO A. GUARINO

SONG

She dwelt among th' untrodden ways
    Beside the springs of Dove:
A maid whom there were none to praise
    And very few to love.

A violet by a mossy stone
    Half-hidden from the eye!
– Fair as a star when only one
    Is shining in the sky!

She lived unknown, and few could know
    When Lucy ceased to be;
But she is in her grave, and oh!
    The difference to me.

WILLIAM WORDSWORTH (1770–1850)

CELANDINE

Thinking of her had saddened me at first,
Until I saw the sun on the celandines lie
Redoubled, and she stood up like a flame,
A living thing, not what before I nursed,
The shadow I was growing to love almost,
The phantom, not the creature with bright eye
That I had thought never to see, once lost.

She found the celandines of February
Always before us all. Her nature and name
Were like those flowers, and now immediately
For a short swift eternity back she came,
Beautiful, happy, simply as when she wore
Her brightest bloom among the winter hues

Of all the world; and I was happy too,
Seeing the blossoms and the maiden who
Had seen them with me Februarys before,
Bending to them as in and out she trod
And laughed, with locks sweeping the mossy sod.

But this was a dream: the flowers were not true,
Until I stooped to pluck from the grass there
One of five petals and I smelt the juice
Which made me sigh, remembering she was no more,
Gone like a never perfectly recalled air.

EDWARD THOMAS (1878–1917)

TO THE SMALL CELANDINE

Pansies, lilies, kingcups, daisies,
Let them live upon their praises;
Long as there's a sun that sets,
Primroses will have their glory;
Long as there are violets,
They will have a place in story:
There's a flower that shall be mine,
'Tis the little Celandine.

Eyes of some men travel far
For the finding of a star;
Up and down the heavens they go,

Men that keep a mighty rout!
I'm as great as they, I trow,
Since the day I found thee out,
Little Flower! – I'll make a stir,
Like a sage astronomer.

Modest, yet withal an Elf
Bold, and lavish of thyself;
Since we needs must first have met
I have seen thee, high and low,
Thirty years or more, and yet
'Twas a face I did not know;
Thou hast now, go where I may,
Fifty greetings in a day.

Ere a leaf is on a bush,
In the time before the thrush
Has a thought about her nest,
Thou wilt come with half a call,
Spreading out thy glossy breast
Like a careless Prodigal;
Telling tales about the sun,
When we've little warmth, or none.

Poets, vain men in their mood!
Travel with the multitude:
Never heed them; I aver
That they all are wanton wooers;
But the thrifty cottager,

Who stirs little out of doors,
Joys to spy thee near her home;
Spring is coming, Thou art come!

Comfort have thou of thy merit,
Kindly, unassuming Spirit!
Careless of thy neighbourhood,
Thou dost show thy pleasant face
On the moor, and in the wood,
In the lane; – there's not a place,
Howsoever mean it be,
But 'tis good enough for thee.

Ill befall the yellow flowers,
Children of the flaring hours!
Buttercups, that will be seen,
Whether we will see or no;
Others, too, of lofty mien;
They have done as worldlings do,
Taken praise that should be thine,
Little, humble Celandine!

Prophet of delight and mirth,
Ill-requited upon earth;
Herald of a mighty band,
Of a joyous train ensuing,
Serving at my heart's command,
Tasks that are no tasks renewing,
I will sing, as doth behove,
Hymns in praise of what I love!

VENUS'S LAMENT FOR ADONIS
From *Metamorphoses*, Book X

'On her light chariot, Venus, who was drawn
across the middle air by her winged swans,
had not reached Cyprus yet; she heard, far off,
the dying boy – his moans. She turned around
her white swans and rode back. When, from the
     heights,
she saw him lifeless there, a bleeding corpse,
she leaped down to the ground. And Venus tore
her hair, and – much unlike a goddess – beat
her hands against her breast. She challenged fate:
 'But destiny does not rule all. Adonis,
your memory will live eternally . . .

'"I shall transform your blood into a flower.
If you, Proserpina, were once allowed
the metamorphosis of Mentha, when
you changed that nymph into a fragrant plant –
the mint – can anyone begrudge me if
I change the form of Cinyras' dear son?"
That said, she sprinkled scented nectar on
his blood, which then fermented, even as
bright bubbles form when raindrops fall on mud.
One hour had yet to pass when, from that gore,
a bloodred flower sprang, the very color
of pomegranates when that fruit is ripe

and hides sweet seeds beneath its pliant rind.
And yet Adonis' blossoms have brief life:
his flower is light and delicate; it clings
too loosely to the stem and thus is called
Anemone – "born of the wind" – because
winds shake its fragile petals, and they fall.'

OVID (43 BC–*c*. AD 17)
TR. ALLEN MANDELBAUM

ANEMONES

Between the flower beds of anemones the breeze of the
    winds was blowing to and fro;

I visited them, while the clouds whipped their flowers
    which shone with the colour of red wine;

I asked: 'What is their fault?' The clouds answered:
    'They have stolen the redness of beautiful cheeks'.

34   IBN AL-ZAQQAQ (*c*. 1096–1134)
    TR. ARIE SCHIPPERS

From SONNETS TO ORPHEUS

Flower-Muscle, with which the anemone
Opens bit by bit in the meadow-morning,
Till into her lap the polyphony
Of the full light of heaven is down-pouring.

In your still, starry blossom, *so* distended
Is your muscle of endless receiving,
Sometimes *such* fullness has descended,
That even the sunset's beckoning

To rest, is scarcely able to give
Back to you the petal-edge, wide-sprung:
You, purpose and strength of *how many* worlds beside

Ours! We, with our violence, longer live.
But *when*, in all our lives, in which one,
Shall we at last, to receive, be open-wide?

RAINER MARIA RILKE (1875–1926)   35
TR. JESSIE LEMONT

PROSERPINA'S FLOWERS
From *The Winter's Tale*, IV.iv

PERDITA [*to Florizel*] Now, my fair'st friend,
I would I had some flow'rs o' th' spring, that might
Become your time of day – [*to Shepherdesses*] and
    yours, and yours,
That wear upon your virgin branches yet
Your maidenheads growing. O Proserpina,
For the flow'rs now, that, frighted, thou let'st fall
From Dis's wagon! Daffodils,
That come before the swallow dares, and take
The winds of March with beauty; violets, dim,
But sweeter than the lids of Juno's eyes,
Or Cytherea's breath; pale primroses,
That die unmarried ere they can behold
Bright Phoebus in his strength (a malady
Most incident to maids); bold oxlips, and
The crown imperial; lilies of all kinds,
The flower-de-luce being one. O, these I lack
To make you garlands of, and my sweet friend,
To strew him o'er and o'er!

FLORIZEL   What, like a corse?

PERDITA No, like a bank for Love to lie and play on,
Not like a corse; or if, not to be buried,
But quick and in mine arms. Come, take your
    flow'rs...

TO PRIMROSES FILLED WITH
MORNING DEW

Why do ye weep, sweet babes? can tears
Speak grief in you,
Who were but born
Just as the modest morn
Teem'd her refreshing dew?
Alas! you have not known that shower
That mars a flower,
Nor felt th' unkind
Breath of a blasting wind,
Nor are ye worn with years,
Or warp'd as we,
Who think it strange to see
Such pretty flowers, like to orphans young,
To speak by tears before ye have a tongue.

ROBERT HERRICK (1591–1674)

THE PRIMROSE BANK

'Tis spring day roams with flowers
Down every little lane
And the night is hardly night
But a round of happy hours.

Yes nights are happy nights
    The sky is full of stars
    Like worlds in peace they lie
Enjoying one delight.

The dew is on the thorn
    And the primrose underneath
    Just again' the mossy root
Is shining to the morn

With its little brunny eye
    And its yellow rim so pale
    And its crimp and curdled leaf—
Who can pass its beauties by

Without a look of love?
    When we tread the little path
    That skirts the woodland side
Who can pass, nor look above

To Him who blesses earth
    With these messengers of spring
    And decorates the fields
For our happiness and mirth?

I cannot for I go
    In my fancy once again
    In the woods and little holts
Where the primrose used to grow;

The wood bank seemed so fair
   And the hedgerow in the lane
   Seemed so sweet that scores of times
Have I wished my cottage there,

And felt that lovely mood
   As a birthright God had given
   To muse in the green woods
And meet the smiles of heaven.

And though no culture comes
   To the places where they grow
   Every spring finds more and more
Till the wood all yellow blooms.

The woodman's guessing way
   Oft tramples many down
   But there's not a blossom missing
When he comes another day.

The woods have happy guests,
   And the birds sing twice as loud
   When they see such crowds of blossoms
Underneath their little nests –

As beauties for the spring –
   Their maker sends them forth
   That man may have his mirth
And nature laugh and sing.

For when roaming where they flower
  They seemed to make woods happy,
  And amid the green light round them
I've spent many a happy hour.

But since I used to stray
  In their hazel haunts for joy,
  The world has found the happy spots
And took the charm away;

It has tracked the pleasant springs
  Like armies on their march,
  Till dearest spots that used to be
Are nought but common things,

Save that their sights employ
  Balm gales and sunny blooms,
  The mind in shaping heavens
As one continued joy.

JOHN CLARE (1793–1864)

BLUE HYACINTHS

In your
Curled petals what ghosts
Of blue headlands and seas,
What perfumed immortal breath sighing
Of Greece.

40 ADELAIDE CRAPSEY (1878–1914)

THE DEATH OF HYACINTHUS
From *Metamorphoses*, Book X

'And you, too, Hyacinthus, would have been
set high within the sky by Phoebus, if
your wretched fate had not forestalled his wish.
Yet, in your way, you are eternal now:
whenever spring has banished winter and
the rainy Fish gives way before the Ram,
it's then you rise and flower once again
where earth is green. My father loved you more
than he loved any other; even Delphi,
set at the very center of the earth,
was left without its tutelary god;
for Phoebus went instead to visit you
in unwalled Sparta, on Eurotas' banks,
neglecting both his lyre and his shafts.
Not heeding who he was – his higher tasks –
alongside you, the god did not refuse
to carry nets, to hold the dogs in leash;
he was your comrade on rough mountain peaks;
and lingering beside you, he could feed
his flame of love.

                    'And now the Titan sun
was at midpoint – between the night to come
and one that had already gone. And Phoebus
and Hyacinthus shed their clothes, anoint

their bodies; gleaming with smooth olive oil,
the two are set to see which one can cast
the discus farther. Phoebus is the first
to lift and poise the broad and heavy disc,
then fling it high; it bursts across the sky
and rends the clouds along its path. Its flight
is long: at last, the hard earth feels its fall,
its weight – a throw that shows what can be done
when strength and skill are joined. The Spartan boy
is reckless: risking all for sport, he runs
to pick the discus up. But the hard ground
sends back the heavy bronze; as it rebounds,
it strikes you in the face, o Hyacinthus!
You and the god are pale: the god lifts up
your sagging form; he tries to warm you, tries
to staunch your cruel wound; and he applies
herbs that might stay your soul as it takes flight.
His arts are useless; nothing now can heal
that wound. As lilies, poppies, violets,
if loosened as they hang from yellow stems
in a well-watered garden, fade at once
and, with their withered heads grown heavy, bend;
they cannot stand erect; instead they must
gaze at the ground: just so your dying face
lies slack: too weak for its own weight, your neck
falls back upon your shoulder. "Sparta's son,
you have been cheated," Phoebus cries; "you've lost

the flower of your youth; as I confront
your wound, I witness my own crime — my guilt,
my grief! It's my right hand that has inscribed
your end: I am the author of your death.
And yet, what crime is mine? Can play, can sport
be blamed? Can having loved be called a fault?
If I could only pay for what I've done
by dying for or with you — you are one
so worthy! But the law of fate denies
that chance to me. Yet I shall always have
you, Hyacinthus, in my heart, just as
your name shall always be upon my lips.
The lyre my fingers pluck, the songs I chant,
shall celebrate you; and as a new flower,
you'll bear, inscribed upon you, my lament.
And, too, in time to come, the bravest man
shall be identified with you — Ajax'
own letters, on your petals, shall be stamped."

'As he spoke these true words, the blood that had
been spilled upon the ground and stained the grass
is blood no more; instead — more brilliant than
the purple dye of Tyre — a flower sprang;
though lily-shaped, it was not silver-white;
this flower was purple. Then, not yet content,
Phoebus — for it was he who'd brought about
this wonder that would honor Hyacinthus —
inscribed upon the petals his lament:

with his own hand, he wrote these letters – AI,
AI – signs of sad outcry. And Sparta, too,
is not ashamed to have as its own son
a Hyacinthus; they still honor him
each year, just as their fathers always did:
the Hyacinthia, their festival,
begins with an august processional.

OVID (43 BC–*c.* AD 17)
TR. ALLEN MANDELBAUM

THE METAMORPHOSIS

Bluebells come crowding a fellside
   A stream once veined. It rises
Like water again where, bell on bell,
   They flow through its bed, each rope
And rivulet, each tributary thread
   Found-out by flowers. And not the slope
Alone, runs with this imaginary water:
   Marshes and pools of it stay
On the valley-floor, fed (so the eye would say)
   From the same store and streamhead.
Like water, too, this blueness not all blue
   Goes ravelled with groundshades, grass and stem,
As the wind dishevels and strokes it open;

So that the mind, in salutary confusion,
Surrendering up its powers to the illusion,
    Could, swimming in metamorphoses, believe
Water itself might move like a flowing of flowers.

CHARLES TOMLINSON (1927–2015)

ECHO'S SONG

Slow, slow, fresh fount, keepe time with my salt teares;
Yet slower, yet, O faintly gentle springs:
List to the heavy part the musique beares,
    Woe weepes out her division, when she sings.
    Droupe hearbs, and flowres;
    Fall griefe in showres;
    Our beauties are not ours:
                            O, I could still
(Like melting snow upon some craggie hill,)
    drop, drop, drop, drop,
Since natures pride is, now, a wither'd daffodill.

BEN JONSON (1572/3–1637)   45

'LOOK NOT IN MY EYES, FOR FEAR'

Look not in my eyes, for fear
    They mirror true the sight I see,
And there you find your face too clear
    And love it and be lost like me.
One the long nights through must lie
    Spent in star-defeated sighs,
But why should you as well as I
    Perish? gaze not in my eyes.

A Grecian lad, as I hear tell,
    One that many loved in vain,
Looked into a forest well
    And never looked away again.
There, when the turf in springtime flowers,
    With downward eye and gazes sad,
Stands amid the glancing showers
    A jonquil, not a Grecian lad.

EYES OF NARCISSI

Is nothing lovelier than narcissus eyes when their
    gazes meet across the gathering?
Pearls have split above a silk brocade, revealing
    emerald-stemmed rubies.
Camphor eyelids are gilded with saffron eyes, soft to
    the touch,
Like moons of night corralling black-bound suns atop
    a supple branch.
In gleaming shadows, tear-filled eyes stare like the
    beholder, intent.
As wind engulfs them, they emit a musky fragrance.
    Oh, what a scent!
Swaying towards each other, they mimic two
    companions drawing near.
The friends fondly embrace in the assembly, just as
    narcissi entwine in the meadow.
As you drowse with wine, the narcissus regards you
    with unsleeping eyes.
Are not narcissi more charming in moonlight than
    daisy and chamomile at sunrise?
O Cup-bearer, your glances tasked with ensnaring
    souls,
You've fixed my heart 'twixt fetching looks and
    scornful words.

AL-SANAWBARI (d. 945)   47
TR. MICHELLE QUAY

Looking, the narcissus, looking.
To blink – what unattained pleasure!
It bows beneath the dewdrop
And, dazed, watches
What the sky is doing to the earth.

ABDALLAH IBN AL-MUʿTAZZ (861–908)

'I WANDERED LONELY AS A CLOUD'

I wandered lonely as a cloud
That floats on high o'er vales and hills,
When all at once I saw a crowd –
A host of dancing daffodils:
Along the lake, beneath the trees,
Ten thousand dancing in the breeze.

The waves beside them danced, but they
Outdid the sparkling waves in glee;
A poet could not but be gay
In such a laughing company.
I gazed – and gazed – but little thought
What wealth the show to me had brought.

For oft when on my couch I lie
In vacant or in pensive mood,
They flash upon that inward eye

Which is the bliss of solitude;
And then my heart with pleasure fills,
And dances with the daffodils.

WILLIAM WORDSWORTH (1770–1850)

DAFFODIL MINISTRY

One of the more difficult denominations.
No artless formula of psalm, collect,
And-now-to-God-the-father; unrelenting ministry
Of the solo conscience. Mankind's cheerless concerns
Can drop in here like friends.

And yet, the daffodils, she says.

And yettishness: a state of mind.

O yes, of course the world is harsh,
And suffering, O yes – and yet
This morning, as I walked along
And saw the daffodils, I thought –
And so forth, daffodilling on.

Easier not to meet each other's eyes.

And yet, and yes, the daffodils
Making their point, in scurfy gardens,
Beside the lake, beneath the trees,

Municipally distributed, like grit.
Wherever a bulb can lodge and multiply,
Long-legged, gape-mouthed, a yellow hop in air,
Daffodils are.
                Homelessness, poverty,
Injustice, executions, arms trade, war
Are too.

The stillness isn't easy with itself.

And yet, and yet.

U. A. FANTHORPE (1929–2009)

TO DAFFODILS

Fair daffodils, we weep to see
    You haste away so soon;
As yet the early-rising sun
    Has not attain'd his noon.
        Stay, stay,
    Until the hasting day
            Has run
        But to the evensong;
And, having prayed together, we
    Will go with you along.

We have short time to stay, as you,
  We have as short a spring;
As quick a growth to meet decay,
  As you, or anything.
      We die,
    As your hours do, and dry
        Away,
    Like to the summer's rain;
Or as the pearls of morning's dew,
  Ne'er to be found again.

ROBERT HERRICK (1591–1674)

From THE DIVAN OF HAFEZ

... What man can tell where Kaus and Kai have gone?
Who knows where even now the restless wind
Scatters the dust of Djem's imperial throne?
And where the tulip, following close behind
The feet of Spring, her scarlet chalice rears,
There Ferhad for the love of Shirin pined,
Dyeing the desert red with his heart's tears.

Bring, bring the cup! drink we while yet we may
To our soul's ruin the forbidden draught;
Perhaps a treasure-trove is hid away
Among those ruins where the wine has laughed! –

Perhaps the tulip knows the fickleness
Of Fortune's smile, for on her stalk's green shaft
She bears a wine-cup through the wilderness . . .

HAFEZ (1320–91)
TR. GERTRUDE BELL

'SOME RAINBOW COMING FROM THE FAIR'

Some rainbow coming from the fair!
Some vision of the World Cashmere
I confidently see!
Or else a peacock's purple train,
Feather by feather, on the plain
Fritters itself away!

The dreamy butterflies bestir,
Lethargic pools resume the whir
Of last year's sundered tune.
From some old fortress on the sun
Baronial bees march, one by one,
In murmuring platoon!

The robins stand as thick to-day
As flakes of snow stood yesterday,
On fence and roof and twig.

The orchis binds her feather on
For her old lover, Don the Sun,
Revisiting the bog!

Without commander, countless, still,
The regiment of wood and hill
In bright detachment stand.
Behold! Whose multitudes are these?
The children of whose turbaned seas,
Or what Circassian land?

EMILY DICKINSON (1830–86)

GHAZAL

What have those tulip-cheeks not done here in the
    garden, yet once more?
Transfixed the striding cypress, made the rose-bud
    speechless as before.

It came a foreigner into the realm of park-lands, thus
    it is
That when the rose holds carnival the tulip's smartly
    shown the door.

Unkindness, yes, and cruelty, are what the Beauties
    practise best;

But they did things to me such as no other lover
　　　ever bore.

His eyebrow bow-like, darts his glances, ah that sweet-
　　　heart still declines
To draw his arrow from my breast so that my pinned-
　　　down heart may soar.

Of Beauties there are thousands, all as fair as Joseph,
　　　yet you'll find
That they do not show off their charms and let
　　　themselves be bidden for.

Thank God for life-enhancing wine and those who
　　　fetch it! Who cares where
Those paradisal springs and founts of life their sundry
　　　waters pour?

Necati, face it, there is precious little such as you
　　　can do;
We are all schooled in suffering by those fair creatures
　　　we adore.

54　NECATI (d. 1509)
　　TR. JOHN R. WALSH

YELLOW TULIPS

Looking into the vase, into the calyx, into the water
    drop,
Looking into the throat of the flower at the pollen
    stain,
I can see the ambush love sprung once in the summery
    wood,
I can see the casualties where they lay, till they set
    forth again.

I can see the lips, parted first in surprise, parted in
    desire,
Smile now as the silence falls on the yellow-dappled
    ride
For each thinks the other can hear each receding
    thought
On each receding tide.

They have come out of the wood now. They are
    skirting the fields
Between the tall wheat and the hedge, on the
    unploughed strips,
And they believe anyone who saw them would know
Every secret of their limbs and of their lips,

As if, like creatures of legend, they had come down out
    of the mist
Back to their native city and stood in the square,

And they were seen to be marked at the throat with a
    certain sign
Whose meaning all could share.

These flowers came from a shop. Really they looked
    nothing much
Till they opened as if in surprise at the heat of
    this hotel.
Then the surprise turned to a shout, and the girl said,
    'Shall I chuck them now
Or give them one more day? They've not lasted so well.'

'Oh give them one more day. They've lasted well
    enough.
They've lasted as love lasts, which is longer than most
    maintain.
Look at the sign it has left here at the throat of the
    flower
And on your tablecloth – look at the pollen stain.'

JAMES FENTON (1949–)

DEATHS OF FLOWERS

I would if I could choose
Age and die outwards as a tulip does;
Not as this iris drawing in, in-coiling
Its complex strange taut inflorescence, willing

Itself a bud again – though all achieved is
No more than a clenched sadness,

The tears of gum not flowing.
I would choose the tulip's reckless way of going;
Whose petals answer light, altering by fractions
From closed to wide, from one through many
        perfections,
Till wrecked, flamboyant, strayed beyond recall,
Like flakes of fire they piecemeal fall.

E. J. SCOVELL (1907–99)

                    Irises –
            from which that rainbow
                .   rises

ISSA (1763–1828)
TR. DAVID G. LANOUE

LOOK DEEP

Look deep into my eyes. Think to yourself,
'There is "the fringèd curtain" where a play
Will shortly be enacted.' Look deep down
Into the pupil. Think, 'I am going to sleep.'

The pupil has its many-tinctured curtain
Of moiré silks, parted to let you in,
And the play will present a goddess you used to know
From the glint of sunlit fountain, from beveled mirror,

A goddess, yes, but only a messenger
Whose message is the armorial fleur-de-lys
She carries in her right hand, signifying
The majesty of France, as handed down

From the royal house of Solomon and David:
Wisdom, music and valor gracefully joined
In trefoil heraldry. Nearly asleep,
You settle down for a full-scale production

Of *The Rainstorm* in its grand entirety,
Which, greater than *The Ring*, lasts forty nights;
Everything huddled in one rocking stateroom,
A saving remnant, a life-raft-world in little.

Dream at your ease of the dark forests of spruce
Swaying in currents of green, gelatinous winds
Above which the classless zoo and zookeepers
Weather the testing and baptismal waters;

Dream of the long, undeviating gloom,
The unrelenting skies, the pounding wet
Through which a peak will thrust, a light, and over
The covenanted ark, an *arc-en-ciel.*

IRIS

a burst of iris so that
come down for
breakfast

we searched through the
rooms for
that

sweetest odor and at
first could not
find its

source then a blue as
of the sea
struck

startling us from among
those trumpeting
petals

THE GILLYFLOWER OF GOLD

A Golden gillyflower to-day
I wore upon my helm alway,
And won the prize of this tourney.
  Hah! hah! la belle jaune giroflée.

However well Sir Giles might sit,
His sun was weak to wither it,
Lord Miles's blood was dew on it:
  Hah! hah! la belle jaune giroflée.

Although my spear in splinters flew
From John's steel-coat, my eye was true;
I wheel'd about, and cried for you,
  Hah! hah! la belle jaune giroflée.

Yea, do not doubt my heart was good,
Though my sword flew like rotten wood,
To shout, although I scarcely stood,
  Hah! hah! la belle jaune giroflée.

My hand was steady, too, to take
My axe from round my neck, and break
John's steel-coat up for my love's sake.
  Hah! hah! la belle jaune giroflée.

When I stood in my tent again,
Arming afresh, I felt a pain
Take hold of me, I was so fain –
  Hah! hah! la belle jaune giroflée.

To hear: *'Honneur aux fils des preux!'*
Right in my ears again, and shew
The gillyflower blossom'd new.
   Hah! hah! la belle jaune giroflée.

The Sieur Guillaume against me came,
His tabard bore three points of flame
From a red heart: with little blame —
   Hah! hah! la belle jaune giroflée —

Our tough spears crackled up like straw;
He was the first to turn and draw
His sword, that had nor speak nor flaw, —
   Hah! hah! la belle jaune giroflée.

But I felt weaker than a maid,
And my brain, dizzied and afraid,
Within my helm a fierce tune play'd, —
   Hah! hah! la belle jaune giroflée.

Until I thought of your dear head,
Bow'd to the gillyflower bed,
The yellow flowers stain'd with red; —
   Hah! hah! la belle jaune giroflée.

Crash! how the swords met, *'giroflée!'*
The fierce tune in my helm would play,
'La belle! la belle jaune giroflée!'
   Hah! hah! la belle jaune giroflée.

Once more the great swords met again,
'La belle! la belle!' but who fell then
Le Sieur Guillaume, who struck down ten; –
  Hah! hah! la belle jaune giroflée.

And as, with maz'd and unarm'd face,
Toward my own crown and the Queen's place
They led me at a gentle pace, –
  Hah! hah! la belle jaune giroflée, –

I almost saw your quiet head
Bow'd o'er the gillyflower bed,
The yellow flowers stain'd with red, –
  Hah! hah! la belle jaune giroflée.[1]

WILLIAM MORRIS (1834–96)

AZALEAS

When you leave,
weary of me,
without a word I shall gently let you go.

From Mt. Yak
in Yŏngbyŏn,
I shall gather armfuls of azaleas
and scatter them on your way.

Step by step
on the flowers placed before you
tread lightly, softly as you go.

When you leave,
weary of me,
though I die, I'll not let one tear fall.

KIM SOWŎL (1902–34)
TR. DAVID R. McCANN

the little shrine
is all azaleas . . .
spring rain

ISSA (1763–1828)
TR. DAVID G. LANOUE

SIGNATURES

False Solomon's Seal —
So called because it lacks a
Star-scar on the heel,

And ends its arched stem
In a spray of white florets,
Later changing them

To a red, not blue,
Spatter of berries – is no
Falser than the true.

Solomon, who raised
The temple and wrote the song,
Wouldn't have dispraised

This bowed, graceful plant
So like an aspergillum,
Nor its variant

With root duly scarred,
Whose bloom-hung stem is like the
Bell-branch of a bard.

Liking best to live
In the deep woods whose light is
Most contemplative,

Both are often found
Where mandrake, wintergreen, and
Dry leaves strew the ground,

Their heads inclining
Toward the dark earth, one blessing
And one divining.

SONNET LX: TO AN AMIABLE GIRL

Miranda! mark where shrinking from the gale,
   Its silken leaves yet moist with early dew,
That fair faint flower, the Lily of the Vale
   Droops its meek head, and looks, methinks, like you!
Wrapp'd in a shadowy veil of tender green,
   Its snowy bells a soft perfume dispense,
And bending as reluctant to be seen,
   In simple loveliness it sooths the sense.
With bosom bared to meet the garish day,
   The glaring Tulip, gaudy, undismay'd,
Offends the eye of taste; that turns away
   To seek the Lily in her fragrant shade.
With such unconscious beauty, pensive, mild,
Miranda charms – Nature's soft modest child.

CHARLOTTE SMITH (1749–1806)

GHAZAL: LILIES OF THE VALLEY

Everywhere we walked we saw lilies of the valley.
Every time we stopped were more lilies of the valley.

Umbrellas passed – fathers, sons,
holding out a hand that bore lilies of the valley.

Every citizen of France
bearing through his own front door lilies of the valley.

But we were out of the know,
though reluctant to ignore lilies of the valley.

Our first May Day in Paris,
knowing nothing of folklore lilies of the valley.

Of Jenny Cook and Chabrol's
buttonhole the night he wore lilies of the valley.

He who sang *Viens poupoule, viens!*
and started the fashion for lilies of the valley.

How fashion then conferred, free
on *les ouvriers* at Dior, lilies of the valley.

Mais nous, sacré bleu, who knew
of charmed *muguets des bois* or lilies of the valley?

And though I wore the perfume
I have always worn before – lilies of the valley

– Diorissimo that is,
no one whispered, 'Meem, *j'adore* lilies of the valley'.

No one made false promises.
And if France did, who blames poor lilies of
      the valley?

THE MERRY MONTH OF MAY
From *The Shepheardes Calender*

Is not thilke the mery moneth of May,
When love lads masken in fresh aray?
How falles it then, we no merrier bene,
Ylike as others, girt in gawdy greene?
Our bloncket liveryes bene all to sadde,
For thilke same season, when all is ycladd
With pleasaunce: the grownd with grasse, the Woods
With greene leaves, the bushes with bloosming Buds.
Yougthes folke now flocken in every where,
To gather may buskets and smelling brere:
And home they hasten the postes to dight,
And all the Kirke pillours eare day light,
With Hawthorne buds, and swete Eglantine,
And girlonds of roses and Sopps in wine.
Such merimake holy Saints doth queme,
But we here sytten as drownd in a dreme.

'THE HAWTHORN HATH
A DEATHLY SMELL'

The flowers of the field
    Have a sweet smell;
Meadowsweet, tansy, thyme,
    And faint-heart pimpernel;
But sweeter even than these,
    The silver of the may
Wreathed is with incense for
    The Judgment Day.

An apple, a child, dust,
    When falls the evening rain,
Wild brier's spicèd leaves,
    Breathe memories again;
With further memory fraught,
    The silver of the may
Wreathed is with incense for
    The Judgment Day.

Eyes of all loveliness –
    Shadow of strange delight,
Even as a flower fades
    Must thou from sight;
But, oh, o'er thy grave's mound,
    Till come the Judgment Day,
Wreathed shall with incense be
    Thy sharp-thorned may.

A BED OF FORGET-ME-NOTS

Is love so prone to change and rot
We are fain to rear Forget-me-not
By measure in a garden plot? –

I love its growth at large and free
By untrod path and unlopped tree,
Or nodding by the unpruned hedge,
Or on the water's dangerous edge
Where flags and meadowsweet blow rank
With rushes on the quaking bank.

Love is not taught in learning's school,
Love is not parcelled out by rule:
Hath curb or call an answer got? –
So free must be Forget-me-not.
Give me the flame no dampness dulls,
The passion of the instinctive pulse,
Love steadfast as a fixèd star,
Tender as doves with nestlings are,
More large than time, more strong than death:
    This all creation travails of –
She groans not for a passing breath –
    This is Forget-me-not and Love.

CHRISTINA ROSSETTI (1830–94)   69

THE COWSLIPS

The dancing Cowslips come in pleasant hours;
Though seldom sung, they're everybody's flowers:
They hurry from the world, and leave the cold;
And all the meadows turn from green to gold:
The shepherd finds them where he went to play,
And wears a nosegay in his mouth all day:
The maiden finds them in the pleasant grove,
And puts them in her bosom with her love;
She loves the ladysmocks: and just beyond
The water blobs close to the meadow-pond.
I've often gone – about where blackthorns stood –
And got the Bedlam-Cowslips in the wood;
Then found the blackbird's nest, and noisy jay
And up and threw the Cowslips all away!

JOHN CLARE (1793–1864)

THE VIRGIN

A crimson rose was she
When she came to me,
A golden buttercup
When I gave her up.

I robbed her of the flame
Of her virgin shame;
She melted, and was spilled,
And my hopes fulfilled.

IBN SA'ID (1210–80)
TR. A. J. ARBERRY

'OH SEE HOW THICK THE GOLDCUP FLOWERS'

Oh see how thick the goldcup flowers
   Are lying in field and lane,
With dandelions to tell the hours
   That never are told again.
Oh may I squire you round the meads
   And pick you posies gay?
'Twill do no harm to take my arm.
   'You may, young man, you may.'

Ah, spring was sent for lass and lad,
   'Tis now the blood runs gold,
And man and maid had best be glad
   Before the world is old.
What flowers to-day may flower to-morrow,
   But never as good as new.

– Suppose I wound my arm right round –
    ''Tis true, young man, 'tis true.'

Some lads there are, 'tis shame to say,
    That only court to thieve,
And once they bear the bloom away
    'Tis little enough they leave.
Then keep your heart for men like me
    And safe from trustless chaps.
My love is true and all for you.
    'Perhaps, young man, perhaps.'

Oh, look in my eyes then, can you doubt?
    – Why, 'tis a mile from town.
How green the grass is all about!
    We might as well sit down.
– Ah, life, what is it but a flower?
    Why must true lovers sigh?
Be kind, have pity, my own, my pretty, –
    'Good-bye, young man, good-bye.'

A. E. HOUSMAN (1859–1936)

TO THE DANDELION

Dear common flower, that grow'st beside the way,
Fringing the dusty road with harmless gold!
    First pledge of blithesome May,

Which children pluck, and, full of pride, uphold –
   High-hearted buccaneers, o'erjoyed that they
An Eldorado in the grass have found,
      Which not the rich earth's ample round
      May match in wealth! – thou art more dear to me
      Than all the prouder summer-blooms may be.

Gold such as thine ne'er drew the Spanish prow
Through the primeval hush of Indian seas;
      Nor wrinkled the lean brow
Of age to rob the lover's heart of ease.
   'T is the spring's largess, which she scatters now
To rich and poor alike, with lavish hand;
      Though most hearts never understand
      To take it at God's value, but pass by
      The offered wealth with unrewarded eye.

Thou art my tropics and mine Italy;
To look at thee unlocks a warmer clime;
      The eyes thou givest me
Are in the heart, and heed not space or time:
   Not in mid June the golden-cuirassed bee
Feels a more summer-like warm ravishment
      In the white lily's breezy tent,
      His conquered Sybaris, than I, when first
      From the dark green thy yellow circles burst.

Then think I of deep shadows on the grass;
Of meadows where in sun the cattle graze,
    Where, as the breezes pass,
The gleaming rushes lean a thousand ways;
    Of leaves that slumber in a cloudy mass,
Or whiten in the wind; of waters blue,
        That from the distance sparkle through
    Some woodland gap; and of a sky above,
    Where one white cloud like a stray lamb doth move.

My childhood's earliest thoughts are linked with thee;
The sight of thee calls back the robin's song,
    Who, from the dark old tree
Beside the door, sang clearly all day long;
    And I, secure in childish piety,
Listened as if I heard an angel sing
        With news from heaven, which he did bring
    Fresh every day to my untainted ears,
    When birds and flowers and I were happy peers.

How like a prodigal doth nature seem
When thou, for all thy gold, so common art!
    Thou teachest me to deem
More sacredly of every human heart,
    Since each reflects in joy its scanty gleam
Of heaven, and could some wondrous secret show,
        Did we but pay the love we owe,
    And with a child's undoubting wisdom look
    On all these living pages of God's book.

DANDYTIME

His gift to me,
the long-forgotten tempo
of a boy's life

as we stop
then start our way
along the old railway

snapping stalks, altering fates
as we go. Not a single clock
will be passed without being blown.

ROY MARSHALL (1966–)

From THE VILLAGE CURATE

          Dandelion this,
A college youth that flashes for a day
All gold; anon he doffs his gaudy suit,
Touch'd by the magic hand of some grave Bishop,
And all at once, by commutation strange,
Becomes a Reverend Divine. How sleek!
How full of grace! and in that globous wig
So nicely trimm'd, unfathomable stores,
No doubt, of erudition most profound:

Each hair is learned, and each awful phiz,
A well-drawn title-page, gives large account
Of matters strangely complicate within.
Place the two doctors each by each, my friends,
Which is the better? say. I blame not you,
Ye powder'd periwigs, that hardly hide,
With glossy suit and well-fed paunch to boot,
The understanding lean and beggarly.
But let me tell you, in the pompous globe
Which rounds the dandelion's head, is couch'd
Divinity most rare. I never pass
But he instructs me with a still discourse
That more persuades than all the vacant noise
Of pulpit rhetoric ...

JAMES HURDIS (1763–1801)

THE DAISY
From *The Legend of Good Women*

Of all the floures in the mede,
Than love I most these floures white and rede,
Soch that men callen daisies in our town;
To hem I have so great affection,
As I said erst, when comen is the May,
That in my bedde there daweth me no day

That I nam up and walking in the mede,
To seene this flour ayenst the Sunne sprede,
Whan it up riseth early by the morrow.
That blissful sight softeneth all my sorrow,
So glad am I, whan that I have the presence
Of it, to done it all reverence,
And ever I love it, and ever ylike newe,
And ever shall, till that mine herte die
All swere I not, of this I will not lie.

My busie gost, that thursteth alway newe,
To seen this flour so yong, so fresh of hew,
Constrained me, with so greedy desire,
That in my herte I fele yet the fire,
That made me rise ere it were day,
And this was now the first morow of May,
With dreadful herte, and glad devotion
For to been at the resurrection
Of this floure, whan that it should unclose
Againe the Sunne, that rose as redde as rose.
And doune on knees anon right I me sette,
And as I could, this fresh floure I grette,
Kneeling alway, till it unclosed was,
Upon the small, soft, swete gras,
That was with floures swete embrouded all,
Of such swetenesse, and such odour overall
That for to speke of gomme, herbe, or tree,
Comparison may not ymaked be,

For it surmounteth plainly all odoures,
And of rich beaute of floures.
And Zephirus, and Flora gentelly,
Yave to these floures soft and tenderly,
His swote breth, and made him for to sprede,
As god and goddesse of the flourie mede,
In which me thoughte I might day by day,
Dwellen alway, the joly month of May,
Withouten slepe, withouten meat or drinke:
Adoune full softly I gan to sinke,
And leaning on my elbow and my side,
The long day I shope me for to abide,
For nothing els, and I shall nat lie,
But for to looke upon the daisie,
That well by reason men it call may
The daisie, or els the eye of the day,
The empress and floure of floures all,
I pray to God that faire mote she fall,
And all that loven floures for her sake.

GEOFFREY CHAUCER (*c.* 1340–1400)

Where innocent bright-eyed daisies are,
    With blades of grass between,
Each daisy stands up like a star
    Out of a sky of green.

CHRISTINA ROSSETTI (1830–94)

TO THE DAISY

Bright Flower! whose home is everywhere,
Bold in maternal Nature's care,
And all the long year through the heir
    Of joy or sorrow;
Methinks that there abides in thee
Some concord with humanity,
Given to no other flower I see
    The forest thorough!

Is it that Man is soon deprest?
A thoughtless Thing! who, once unblest,
Does little on his memory rest,
    Or on his reason,
And Thou would'st teach him how to find
A shelter under every wind,
A hope for times that are unkind
    And every season?

Thou wander'st the wide world about,
Unchecked by pride or scrupulous doubt,
With friends to greet thee, or without,
    Yet pleased and willing;
Meek, yielding to the occasion's call,
And all things suffering from all
Thy function apostolical
    In peace fulfilling.

'SO HAS A DAISY VANISHED'

So has a daisy vanished
From the fields today,
So tiptoed many a slipper
To paradise away,

Oozed so in crimson bubbles
Day's departing tide,
Blooming, tripping, flowing –
Are ye then with God?

EMILY DICKINSON (1830–86)

A DAISY

Look unoriginal
Being numerous. They ask for attention
With that gradated yellow swelling
Of oily stamens. Petals focus them:
The eye-lashes grow wide.
Why should not one bring these to a funeral?
And at night, like children,
Without anxiety, their consciousness
Shut with white petals.

Blithe, individual.

The unwearying, small sunflower
Fills the grass
With versions of one eye.
A strength in the full look
Candid, solid, glad.
Domestic as milk.

In multitudes, wait,
Each, to be looked at, spoken to.
They do not wither;
Their going, a pressure
Of elate sympathy
Released from you.

Rich up to the last interval
With minute tubes of oil, pollen;
Utterly without scent, for the eye,
For the eye, simply. For the mind
And its invisible organ,
That feeling thing.

MARGUERITE

Shining marguerite,
Flower fair and sweet,
Golden glow a-glimmer
On your silver shimmer.

Frankish slave, pale-faced,
Magian faith embraced,
Mystic fire discerning,
To its altar turning.

Mouth of my adored,
And, for love's reward,
Gleaming gold I shower
In her mouth, my flower.

IBN BILLITA (d. 1048)
TR. A. J. ARBERRY

MOCK ORANGE

It is not the moon, I tell you.
It is these flowers
lighting the yard.

I hate them.
I hate them as I hate sex,

the man's mouth
sealing my mouth, the man's
paralyzing body –

and the cry that always escapes,
the low, humiliating
premise of union –

In my mind tonight
I hear the question and pursuing answer
fused in one sound
that mounts and mounts and then
is split into the old selves,
the tired antagonisms. Do you see?
We were made fools of.
And the scent of mock orange
drifts through the window.

How can I rest?
How can I be content
when there is still
that odor in the world?

PEONY
From *Hortorum libri IV*

    Erect in all her scarlet Pomp you'll see
With bushy Leaves the graceful Peony;
Whose Blushes might the Praise of Virtue claim,
But her vile Scent betrays they rise from Shame;
Happy her Form and innocent her Red,
If while *Alcinous* bleating Flock she fed,
A heav'nly Lover had not sought her Bed;
Shy of Mankind her Pride preserv'd her just,
And Pride betray'd her to *Apollo*'s Lust.

RENÉ RAPIN (1621–87)
TR. JAMES GARDINER

RED PEONIES

    Such radiance of green,
        so casual and composed;
The tint of her dress
        blends crimson with pink.
The heart of a flower
        is nearly torn with grief:
Will spring's brilliance
        ever know her heart?

WANG WEI (701–61)
TR. IRVING Y. LO

Sadness at twilight...
villain! I have
let my hand
cut that peony

BUSON (1716—84)
TR. PETER BEILENSON

PEONIES AT JIXING TEMPLE

Springtime radiance, gradually, gradually where does
    it go?
Again before a wine jar, we take up a goblet.
All day we've questioned the flowers, but the flowers
    do not speak.
For whom do they shed their petals and leaves, for
    whom do they bloom?

LILIES AND ROSES

For, in the flaxen Lillies shade,
It like a bank of Lillies laid.
Upon the Roses it would feed,
Until its Lips ev'n seem'd to bleed:
And then to me 'twould boldly trip,
And print those Roses on my Lip.
But all its chief delight was still
On Roses thus its self to fill:
And its pure virgin Limbs to fold
In whitest sheets of Lillies cold.
Had it liv'd long, it would have been
Lillies without, Roses within.

ANDREW MARVELL
THE NYMPH COMPLAINING FOR
THE DEATH OF HER FAUN

LILIES

The hands of spring
have built crenellated castles
atop the lily stalks:

silver parapets
where knights defend the prince
with golden swords.

IBN DARRAJ AL-QASTALLI (958–1030)
TR. COLA FRANZEN

From *BALIN AND BALAN*

Then chanced, one morning, that Sir Balin sat
Close-bower'd in that garden nigh the hall.
A walk of roses ran from door to door;
A walk of lilies crost it to the bower:
And down that range of roses the great Queen
Came with slow steps, the morning on her face;
And all in shadow from the counter door
Sir Lancelot as to meet her, then at once,
As if he saw not, glanced aside, and paced
The long white walk of lilies toward the bower.
Follow'd the Queen; Sir Balin heard her 'Prince,
Art thou so little loyal to thy Queen,

As pass without good morrow to thy Queen?'
To whom Sir Lancelot with his eyes on earth,
'Fain would I still be loyal to the Queen.'
'Yea so' she said 'but so to pass me by –
So loyal scarce is loyal to thyself,
Whom all men rate the king of courtesy.
Let be: ye stand, fair lord, as in a dream.'

Then Lancelot with his hand among the flowers
'Yea – for a dream. Last night methought I saw
That maiden Saint who stands with lily in hand
In yonder shrine. All round her prest the dark,
And all the light upon her silver face
Flow'd from the spiritual lily that she held.
Lo! these her emblems drew mine eyes – away:
For see, how perfect-pure! As light a flush
As hardly tints the blossom of the quince
Would mar their charm of stainless maidenhood.'

'Sweeter to me' she said 'this garden rose
Deep-hued and many-folded! sweeter still
The wild-wood hyacinth and the bloom of May.
Prince, we have ridd'n before among the flowers
In those fair days – not all as cool as these,
Tho' season-earlier. Art thou sad? or sick?
Our noble King will send thee his own leech –
Sick? or for any matter anger'd at me?'

MARY'S GIRLHOOD

This is that blessed Mary, pre-elect
   God's Virgin. Gone is a great while, and she
   Dwelt young in Nazareth of Galilee.
Unto God's will she brought devout respect,
Profound simplicity of intellect,
   And supreme patience. From her mother's knee
   Faithful and hopeful; wise in charity;
Strong in grave peace; in pity circumspect.

So held she through her girlhood; as it were
   An angel-watered lily, that near God
     Grows and is quiet. Till, one dawn at home
She woke in her white bed, and had no fear
   At all, – yet wept till sunshine, and felt awed:
     Because the fulness of the time was come.

DANTE GABRIEL ROSSETTI (1828–82)

THE LILLY

The modest Rose puts forth a thorn,
The humble Sheep a threat'ning horn,
While the Lilly white shall in Love delight,
Nor a thorn nor a threat stain her beauty bright.

WILLIAM BLAKE (1757–1827)

THE LILY IN A CRYSTAL

You have beheld a smiling rose
    When virgins' hands have drawn
    O'er it a cobweb-lawn;
And here you see this lily shows,
    Tomb'd in a crystal stone,
More fair in this transparent case
    Than when it grew alone
    And had but single grace.

You see how cream but naked is
    Nor dances in the eye
    Without a strawberry,
Or some fine tincture like to this,
    Which draws the sight thereto
More by that wantoning with it
    Than when the paler hue
    No mixture did admit.

You see how amber through the streams
    More gently strokes the sight
    With some conceal'd delight
Than when he darts his radiant beams
    Into the boundless air;
Where either too much light is worth
    Doth all at once impair,
    Or set it little forth.

Put purple grapes or cherries in-
    To glass, and they will send
    More beauty to commend
Them from that clean and subtle skin
    Than if they naked stood,
And had no other pride at all
    But their own flesh and blood
    And tinctures natural.

Thus lily, rose, grape, cherry, cream,
    And strawberry do stir
    More love when they transfer
A weak, a soft, a broken beam,
    Than if they should discover
At full their proper excellence;
    Without some scene cast over
    To juggle with the sense.

Thus let this crystal'd lily be
    A rule how far to teach
    Your nakedness must reach;
And that no further than we see
    Those glaring colours laid
By art's wise hand, but to this end
    They should obey a shade,
    Lest they too far extend.

So though you're white as swan or snow,
    And have the power to move
    A world of men to love,

Yet when your lawns and silks shall flow,
    And that white cloud divide
Into a doubtful twilight, then,
        Then will your hidden pride
        Raise greater fires in men.

ROBERT HERRICK (1591–1674)

MATTHEW 6:28–9

And why take ye thought for raiment? Consider the
lilies of the field, how they grow; they toil not, neither
do they spin.
And yet I say unto you, that even Solomon in all his
glory was not arrayed like one of these.

THE NEW TESTAMENT (KING JAMES VERSION)

SONG OF THE ENCHANTRESS
From *Faerie Queene*, Book II

Behold, O man, that toilesome paines doest take,
    The flowres, the fields, and all that pleasant growes,
    How they themselves doe thine ensample make,

Whiles nothing envious nature them forth throwes
Out of her fruitfull lap; how, no man knowes,
They spring, they bud, they blossome fresh and
    faire,
And deck the world with their rich pompous
    showes;
Yet no man for them taketh paines or care,
Yet no man to them can his carefull paines compare.

The lilly, Ladie of the flowring field,
    The Flowre-deluce, her lovely Paramoure,
    Bid thee to them thy fruitlesse labours yield,
    And soone leave off this toylesome wearie stoure;
    Loe loe how brave she decks her bounteous boure,
    With silken curtens and gold coverlets,
    Therein to shrowd her sumptuous Belamoure,
    Yet neither spinnes nor cardes, ne cares nor frets,
But to her mother Nature all her care she lets.

Why then dost thou, O man, that of them all
    Art Lord, and eke of nature Soveraine,
    Wilfully make thy selfe a wretched thrall,
    And wast thy joyous houres in needlesse paine,
    Seeking for daunger and adventures vaine?
    What bootes it all to have, and nothing use?
    Who shall him rew, that swimming in the maine,
    Will die for thirst, and water doth refuse?
Refuse such fruitlesse toile, and present pleasures
    chuse.

EDMUND SPENSER (c. 1552–99)   95

THE SILVER LILY

The nights have grown cool again, like the nights
of early spring, and quiet again. Will
speech disturb you? We're
alone now; we have no reason for silence.

Can you see, over the garden — the full moon rises.
I won't see the next full moon.

In spring, when the moon rose, it meant
time was endless. Snowdrops
opened and closed, the clustered
seeds of the maples fell in pale drifts.
White over white, the moon rose over the birch tree.
And in the crook, where the tree divides,
leaves of the first daffodils, in moonlight
soft greenish-silver.

We have come too far together toward the end now
to fear the end. These nights, I am no longer even
        certain
I know what the end means. And you, who've been
        with a man —

after the first cries,
doesn't joy, like fear, make no sound?

REQUIESCAT

Tread lightly, she is near
 Under the snow,
Speak gently, she can hear
 The daisies grow.

All her bright golden hair
 Tarnished with rust,
She that was young and fair
 Fallen to dust.

Lily-like, white as snow,
 She hardly knew
She was a woman, so
 Sweetly she grew.

Coffin-board, heavy stone,
 Lie on her breast,
I vex my heart alone,
 She is at rest.

Peace, Peace, she cannot hear
 Lyre or sonnet,
All my life's buried here,
 Heap earth upon it.

'THROUGH THE DARK SOD'

Through the dark sod
As education,
The Lily passes sure,
Feels her white foot
No trepidation,
Her faith no fear.

Afterward in the meadow
Swinging her beryl bell,
The mold-life all forgotten now –
In ecstasy and dell.

EMILY DICKINSON (1830–86)

LILIES AND WINE

The white and gold flowers and the wine,
Symbols of all that is not mine,
Stand sacramental, and so bless
The wounded mind with loveliness
That it leaps blindly to evade
The world's anguish there portrayed.
What of the water and the green?
I know what leaves and water mean –

The bright blade and the limpid flow,
I knew and loved them long ago;
But now the white, the gold, the blood
Dawn doomlike, not to be withstood.

At the white, gold, and crimson gate
I and my heart stand still and wait.

RUTH PITTER (1897–1992)

＊

The rose is without why, it blooms because it blooms,
It pays no attention to itself, asks not whether it is seen.

ANGELUS SILESIUS (*c.* 1624–77)

LEUCIPPE'S SONG
From *Cleitophon and Leucippe*

'If Zeus had wished to give the flowers a king, that
king would have been the rose; for it is the ornament
of the world, the glory of the plants, the eye of all
flowers, the meadows' blush, beauty itself glowing; it
has the breath of Love, it is the go-between of Aphro-
dite; its foliage is of sweet-smelling leaves, it glories in
its rustling petals which seem to smile at the approach

of the Zephyr.' Thus she sang; but to me it seemed as if I saw that rose upon her lips, as it were a flower converted into the shape of her sweet mouth.

ACHILLES TATIUS (*fl. c.* 2ND CENTURY AD)
TR. STEPHEN GASELEE

The rose – a rich gift, angel-brought from Paradise!
In the midst of rose-delights, man's soul more noble
    grows.
Ah, rose-seller! How canst for silver sell,
Or what for silver buy more precious than the rose?

KISA'I (953–after 1000)
TR. A. V. WILLIAMS JACKSON

THE ROSE

Today is a spring day, a day of joy and happiness. This year where the roses bloom more than usual is the year of the roses.

In this season of spring our state and condition are very good. May the state and condition of the rose be good as well.

Help has arrived from beyond, from the rose garden

of the Friend's face. Therefore, our eyes won't see the rose wither and its leaves falling.

Everybody's eyes are in awe before the rose's beauty, elegance, magnificence, color, and smell. In the garden it is smiling with its beautiful mouth. Sesame is whispering the secrets of the nightingale's love and the virtues of the rose into the ear of the cypress tree.

In order to do us a favor, to make us sense its fragrance better, the rose has come to us running and tearing its clothes. We, too, are tearing our clothes because we have reunited with the rose, and we want to be closer to the rose.

The rose has come from beyond; it is from the other world. That's why this world cannot encompass the rose.

The rose is so graceful, so elegant that the world of dreams is too narrow to dream of the rose.

Who is meant by 'the rose'? A messenger from the garden of the intellect, from the grove of spirit? What is 'the rose'? A document that describes the beauty and the highness of the rose of truth that neither turns brown nor withers.

Let us hold onto the rose's skirt and be its fellow traveler so that we may journey happily to the origin of the rose, the everlasting rose shoot.

The origin of the rose, the everlasting rose shoot, has sprung from the sweat of Mustafa, peace and blessings be upon him, and has grown from His grace.

Thanks to that Gracious Being, it turned from a crescent to a full moon. You may pluck the rose's leaves and break its branches and yet they grant it a new spirit, a new life, they bestow it with hands and wings.

See how the rose has answered the invitation of the spring. Just like Abraham's, the Friend of God, four pigeons that were resurrected after being killed and returned to their master.

O Master, be silent! Don't open your lips. Sit in the rose's shadow and just like the rosebud; secretly smile with your lips.

RUMI (1207–73)
TR. ZEKI SARITOPRAK

From *THE ROSES*

A single rose is every rose
and this one: irreplaceable,
perfect, a supple vocable
by the text of things enclosed.

Without her, how can we ever
talk about what our hopes were,
about the tender intervals
in this perpetual departure.

Let's not speak of you. Ineffable.
That is your nature.
Other flowers decorate the table
you transfigure.

We put you in a simple vase —
everything is mutable;
perhaps it's the same phrase,
but now sung by an angel.

RAINER MARIA RILKE (1875–1926)
TR. A. POULIN, JR.

'THERE IS NO ROSE'

There is no rose of swich vertu
As is the rose that bare Jhesu.
    Alleluia.

For in this rose conteynyd was
Heven and erthe in lytyl space,
    Res miranda.

Be that rose we may weel see
That he is God in personys three,
    Pari forma.

The aungelys sungyn the shepherdes to
'Gloria in excelcis Deo.'
　　　Gaudeamus.

Leve we all this wordly merthe,
And folwe we this joyful berthe;
　　　Transeamus.

ANON. (15TH CENTURY)

ON NEWBLOWN ROSES

Spring, and the sharpness of the golden dawn.
Before the sun was up a cooler breeze
Had blown, in promise of a day of heat,
And I was walking in my formal garden,
To freshen me, before the day grew old.

I saw the hoar frost stiff on the bent grasses,
Sitting in fat globes on the cabbage leaves,
And all my Paestum roses laughing at me,
Dew-drenched, and in the East the morning star,
And here and there a dewdrop glistening white,
That soon must perish in the early sun.

Think you, did Dawn steal colour from the roses,
Or was it new born day that stained the rose?

To each one dew, one crimson, and one morning,
To star and rose, their lady Venus one.
Mayhap one fragrance, but the sweet of Dawn
Drifts through the sky, and closer breathes the rose.

A moment dies: this bud that was new born
Has burgeoned even fold on even fold;
This still is green, with her close cap of leaves,
This shows a red stain on her tender sheath,
This the first crimson of the loosened bud;
And now she thinks to unwind her coverings,
And lo! the glory of the radiant chalice,
Scatt'ring the close seeds of her golden heart.
One moment, all on fire and crimson glowing,
All pallid now and bare and desolate.
I marvelled at the flying rape of time;
But now a rose was born: that rose is old.
Even as I speak the crimson petals float
Down drifting, and the crimsoned earth is bright.

So many lovely things, so rare, so young,
A day begat them, and a day will end.
O Earth, to give a flower so brief a grace!
As long as a day is long, so long the life of a rose.
The golden sun at morning sees her born,
And late at eve returning finds her old.
Yet wise is she, that hath so soon to die,

And lives her life in some succeeding rose.
O maid, while youth is with the rose and thee,
Pluck thou the rose: life is as swift for thee.

AUSONIUS (*c.* 310–*c.* 393)
TR. HELEN WADDELL

GO, LOVELY ROSE

Go, lovely Rose –
    Tell her that wastes her time and me,
    That now she knows,
When I resemble her to thee,
How sweet and fair she seems to be.

    Tell her that's young,
And shuns to have her graces spied,
    That hadst thou sprung
In deserts where no men abide,
Thou must have uncommended died.

    Small is the worth
Of beauty from the light retired:
    Bid her come forth,
Suffer herself to be desired,
And not blush so to be admired.

          Then die – that she
The common fate of all things rare
          May read in thee;
How small a part of time they share
That are so wondrous sweet and fair!

EDMUND WALLER (1606–87)

ON A ROSEBUD SENT TO HER LOVER

The tender bud within herself doth close
With secret sweetness till it prove a rose;
And then as fit for profit as for pleasure
Yields sweet content to him that gains the treasure:
          So she that sent this, yet a bud unblown,
          In time may prove a rose, and be your own.

ANON. (c. 1640s)

UPON ROSES

Under a lawn, than skies more clear,
Some ruffled roses nestling were:
And snugging there, they seem'd to lie
As in a flowery nunnery:

They blush'd, and look'd more fresh than flowers
Quicken'd of late by pearly showers,
And all because they were possess'd
But of the heat of Julia's breast:
Which, as a warm and moisten'd spring,
Gave them their ever-flourishing.

ROBERT HERRICK (1591–1674)

THE NIGHTINGALE AND THE ROSE

I walked within a garden fair
At dawn, to gather roses there;
When suddenly sounded in the dale
The singing of a nightingale.

Alas, he loved a rose, like me,
And he, too, loved in agony;
Tumbling upon the mead he sent
The cataract of his lament.

With sad and meditative pace
I wandered in that flowery place,
And thought upon the tragic tale
Of love, and rose, and nightingale.

The rose was lovely, as I tell;
The nightingale he loved her well;
He with no other love could live,
And she no kindly word would give.

It moved me strangely, as I heard
The singing of that passionate bird;
So much it moved me, I could not
Endure the burden of his throat.

Full many a fair and fragrant rose
Within the garden freshly blows,
Yet not a bloom was ever torn
Without the wounding of the thorn.

Think not, O Hafez, any cheer
To gain of Fortune's wheeling sphere;
Fate has a thousand turns of ill,
And never a tremor of good will.

HAFEZ (1320–91)
TR. A. J. ARBERRY

ROSEBUD IN THE HEATHER

Urchin saw a rose – a dear
Rosebud in the heather.
Fresh as dawn and morning-clear;
Ran up quick and stooped to peer,
Took his fill of pleasure,
Rosebud, rosebud, rosebud red,
Rosebud in the heather.

Urchin blurts: 'I'll pick you, though,
Rosebud in the heather!'
Rosebud: 'Then I'll stick you so
That there's no forgetting, no!
I'll not stand it, ever!'
Rosebud, rosebud, rosebud red,
Rosebud in the heather.

But the wild young fellow's torn
Rosebud from the heather.
Rose, she pricks him with her thorn;
Should she plead, or cry forlorn?
Makes no difference whether.
Rosebud, rosebud, rosebud red,
Rosebud in the heather.

THE SICK ROSE

O rose, thou art sick:
The invisible worm
That flies in the night
In the howling storm,

Has found out thy bed
Of crimson joy,
And his dark secret love
Does thy life destroy.

WILLIAM BLAKE (1757–1827)

SONNET CXLVII
In which she morally censures a rose,
and thereby all that resemble it

O rose divine, in gentle cultivation
you are, with all your fragrant subtlety,
tuition, purple-hued, to loveliness,
snow-white instruction to the beautiful;

intimation of a human structure,
example of gentility in vain,
to whose one being nature has united
the joyful cradle and the mournful grave;

how haughty in your pomp, presumptuous one,
how proud when you disdain the threat of death,
then, in a swoon and shriveling, you give

a withered vision of a failing self;
and so, with your wise death and foolish life,
in living you deceive, dying you teach!

SOR JUANA INÉS DE LA CRUZ (1651–95)
TR. EDITH GROSSMAN

A WHITE ROSE

I have a white rose to tend
In July as in January;
I give it to the true friend
Who offers his frank hand to me.
And for the cruel one whose blows
Break the heart by which I live,
Thistle nor thorn do I give:
For him, too, I have a white rose.

112 JOSÉ MARTÍ (1853–95)
TR. MANUEL A. TELLECHEA

MY PRETTY ROSE TREE

A flower was offer'd to me,
Such a flower as May never bore;
But I said 'I've a Pretty Rose-tree,'
And I passed the sweet flower o'er.

Then I went to my Pretty Rose-tree,
To tend her by day and by night;
But my Rose turn'd away with jealousy,
And her thorns were my only delight.

WILLIAM BLAKE (1757–1827)

AMONG HIS BOOKS

A silent room – gray with a dusty blight
    Of loneliness;
A room with not enough of life or light
    Its form to dress.

Books enough though! The groaning sofa bears
    A goodly store –
Books on the window-seat, and on the chairs,
    And on the floor.

Books of all sorts of soul, all sorts of age,
    All sorts of face –
Black-letter, vellum, and the flimsy page
    Of commonplace.

All bindings, from the cloth whose hue distracts
    One's weary nerves,
To yellow parchment, binding rare old tracts
    It serves – deserves.

Books on the shelves, and in the cupboard books,
    Worthless and rare –
Books on the mantelpiece – where'er one looks
    Books everywhere!

Books! books! the only things in life I find
    Not wholly vain.
Books in my hands – books in my heart enshrined –
    Books in my brain.

My friends are they: for children and for wife
    They serve me too;
For these alone, of all dear things in life,
    Have I found true.

They do not flatter, change, deny, deceive –
    Ah no – not they!
The same editions which one night you leave
    You find next day.

You don't find railway novels where you left
    Your Elzevirs!
Your Aldines don't betray you – leave bereft
    Your lonely years!

And yet this common Book of Common Prayer
    My heart prefers,
Because the names upon the fly-leaf there
    Are mine and hers.

It's a dead flower that makes it open so –
    Forget-me-not –
The Marriage Service … well, my dear, you know
    Who first forgot.

Those were the days when in the choir we two
    Sat – used to sing –
When I believed in God, in love, in you –
    In everything.

Through quiet lanes to church we used to come,
    Happy and good,
Clasp hands through sermon, and go slowly home
    Down through the wood.

Kisses? A certain yellow rose no doubt
    That porch still shows;
Whenever I hear kisses talked about,
    I smell that rose!

No – I don't blame you – since you only proved
    My choice unwise,
And taught me books should trusted be and loved,
    Not lips and eyes!

And so I keep your book – your flower – to show
    How much I care
For the dear memory of what, you know,
    You never were.

E. NESBIT (1858–1924)

INJUDICIOUS GARDENING[2]

If yellow betokens infidelity,
    I am an infidel.
        I could not bear a yellow rose ill will
        Because books said that yellow boded ill,
    White promised well;

However, your particular possession –
    The sense of privacy
        In what you did – deflects from your estate
        Offending eyes, and will not tolerate
    Effrontery.

From *GARDENERS ALL*

Here, looking just a little sad,
(Most men of fifty do) is Dad,
Eyeing the roses with an air
Like the faint ghost of love's despair.
To such a pass romantics come
After they've been and married Mum,
And youthful dreams must go repose
Under their monument, the rose.
Perverse old Dad! you've got a wife
Who is a cushion to your life,
Housekeeps so well, and mends, and cooks,
Is kind, and not so bad for looks;
And such a mother! where could be
A batch of kids to beat your three?
But still the old unsatisfied
Visions within the heart abide;
And since you are not really bad,
No wicked, dissipated Dad;
Since you don't reason much, nor wholly
Identify your melancholy,
Love's face has dreamed itself into
This perfect Rose, a queen to you.

RONDEAU

Give me a rose, cool-petaled, virgin white,
Pure as the morning, mystical as night;
    Not bold gardenias, flaunting their expense
    Like courtesans, in perfumed insolence,
Nor brazen orchids, feverishly bright.

Give me no hothouse violets, cold, polite,
With lengths of costly ribbon girdled tight –
    Matrons, in corseted magnificence;
                Give me a rose.

One girlish blossom proffer as your mite.
Ah, lovelier by far within my sight
    Than rich exotics' glamorous pretense
    Is one shy rose, sweet in its diffidence.
And then besides, my love, the price is right;
                Give me a rose.

THE TEA-ROSE

Of all the roses, surely must
The tea-rose be the daintiest:
Her leaves half-closed, her bud is just
A slightly crimsoned hue at best.

One might indeed even suppose
She were a white rose – blushing, shy –
Tweaked on the twig by one of those:
An all-too-amorous butterfly!

Her fabric pink, diaphanous –
Bloom of flesh-tinted velvet, she.
All other reds beside her, thus,
Fade or turn vulgar frippery.

Her hue, aristocratic, pure ...
Such that her sisters' sun-bronzed skin
Seems almost dark as rustic boor,
Though warm its rich incarnadine.

Yet, at some ball, if your hand goes
To breathe her scent, and gently brings
Her to your cheek, this lustrous rose
Becomes the most banal of things.

No rose is there – my love, my sweet –
Born of spring's tender palette green,
That would dare venture to compete
Against your seasons seventeen.

Ah! Better flesh than petals, surely!
And blood of noble heart well-bred
Spread over youthful beauty purely,
Bests every other pink and red!

THÉOPHILE GAUTIER (1811–72)
TR. NORMAN R. SHAPIRO

SEA ROSE

Rose, harsh rose,
marred and with stint of petals,
meagre flower, thin,
sparse of leaf,

more precious
than a wet rose
single on a stem –
you are caught in the drift.

Stunted, with small leaf,
you are flung on the sand,
you are lifted

in the crisp sand
that drives in the wind.

Can the spice-rose
drip such acrid fragrance
hardened in a leaf?

H. D. (HILDA DOOLITTLE) (1911–61)

TO THE ROSE UPON THE ROOD OF TIME

Red Rose, proud Rose, sad Rose of all my days!
Come near me, while I sing the ancient ways:
Cuchulain battling with the bitter tide;
The Druid, grey, wood-nurtured, quiet-eyed,
Who cast round Fergus dreams, and ruin untold;
And thine own sadness, whereof stars, grown old
In dancing silver-sandalled on the sea,
Sing in their high and lonely melody.
Come near, that no more blinded by man's fate,
I find under the boughs of love and hate,
In all poor foolish things that live a day,
Eternal beauty wandering on her way.

Come near, come near, come near – Ah, leave me still
A little space for the rose-breath to fill!
Lest I no more hear common things that crave;
The weak worm hiding down in its small cave,

The field-mouse running by me in the grass,
And heavy mortal hopes that toil and pass;
But seek alone to hear the strange things said
By God to the bright hearts of those long dead,
And learn to chaunt a tongue men do not know.
Come near; I would, before my time to go,
Sing of old Eire and the ancient ways:
Red Rose, proud Rose, sad Rose of all my days.

w. b. yeats (1865–1939)

A ROSE AND MILTON

From all the generations of past roses,
Disintegrated in the depths of time,
I want one to be spared oblivion –
One unexceptional rose from all the things
That once existed. Destiny allows me
The privilege of choosing, this first time,
That silent flower, the very final rose
That Milton held before his face, but could
Not see. O rose, vermilion or yellow
Or white, from some obliterated garden,
Your past existence magically lasts
And glows forever in this poetry,
Gold or blood-covered, ivory or shadowed,
As once in Milton's hands, invisible rose.

122 jorge luis borges (1899–1986)
   tr. alastair reid

SUMMER

The striped carnation, and the guarded rose,
The vulgar wall-flower, and smart gillyflower,
The polyanthus mean – the dapper daisy,
Sweet William, and sweet marjoram – and all
The tribe of single and of double pinks!

RICHARD BRINSLEY SHERIDAN
THE CRITIC

SONNET LXIV

Comming to kisse her lyps, (such grace I found)
   Me seemd I smelt a gardin of sweet flowres:
   that dainty odours from them threw around
   for damzels fit to decke their lovers bowres.
Her lips did smell lyke unto Gillyflowers,
   her ruddy cheekes lyke unto Roses red:
   her snowy browes lyke budded Bellamoures,
   her lovely eyes lyke Pincks but newly spred.
Her goodly bosome lyke a Strawberry bed,
   her neck lyke to a bounch of Cullambynes:
   her brest lyke lillyes, ere theyr leaves be shed,
   her nipples lyke yong blossomd Jessemynes.
Such fragrant flowres doe give most odorous smell,
   but her sweet odour did them all excell.

EDMUND SPENSER (*c.* 1552–99)

MADONNA OF THE EVENING FLOWERS

All day long I have been working,
Now I am tired.
I call: 'Where are you?'
But there is only the oak tree rustling in the wind.
The house is very quiet,

The sun shines in on your books,
On your scissors and thimble just put down,
But you are not there.
Suddenly I am lonely:
Where are you?
I go about searching.

Then I see you,
Standing under a spire of pale blue larkspur,
With a basket of roses on your arm.
You are cool, like silver,
And you smile.
I think the Canterbury bells are playing little tunes.

You tell me that the peonies need spraying,
That the columbines have overrun all bounds,
That the pyrus japonica should be cut back and
    rounded.
You tell me these things.
But I look at you, heart of silver,
White heart-flame of polished silver,
Burning beneath the blue steeples of the larkspur.
And I long to kneel instantly at your feet,
While all about us peal the loud, sweet *Te Deums* of
    the Canterbury bells.

LOVE IN A MIST

Light love in a mist, by the midsummer moon mis-
    guided,
Scarce seen in the twilight garden if gloom insist,
Seems vainly to seek for a star whose gleam has
    derided
        Light love in a mist.

All day in the sun, when the breezes do all they list,
His soft blue raiment of cloudlike blossom abided
Unrent and unwithered of winds and of rays that
    kissed.

Blithe-hearted or sad, as the cloud or the sun subsided,
Love smiled in the flower with a meaning whereof
    none wist
Save two that beheld, as a gleam that before them
    glided,
        Light love in a mist.

NIGHT VIOLET[3]

Not long ago along this woodland ride
The rain paced, like a surveyor. Here,
Lily of the valley is bowed with spoon-bait,
And water hides in the mullein's ear.

Their lobes in a pine-root cradle
Are burdened with dew at dusk.
They dislike the daylight. Each grows by itself
And gives off its own sweet musk.

When people are drinking tea in their dachas,
Mist releases the mosquito fleet,
And night, unexpectedly strumming a tune
On the moon, stands blanched in the wheat,

Then everything smells of night violets:
Summers and faces and thoughts. All events
That can be salvaged from the past
And those the future has still to dispense.

NOON AND NIGHT FLOWER

Not any flower that blows
But shining watch doth keep;
Every swift changing chequered hour it knows
Now to break forth in beauty; now to sleep.

This for the roving bee
Keeps open house, and this
Stainless and clear is, that in darkness she
May lure the moth to where her nectar is.

Lovely beyond the rest
Are these of all delight: —
The tiny pimpernel that noon loves best,
The primrose palely burning through the night.

One 'neath day's burning sky
With ruby decks her place,
The other when eve's chariot glideth by
Lifts her dim torch to light that dreaming face.

THE EVENING PRIMROSE

You know the bloom, unearthly white,
That none has seen by morning light –
The tender moon, alone, may bare
Its beauty to the secret air.
Who'd venture past its dark retreat
Must kneel, for holy things and sweet.
That blossom, mystically blown,
No man may gather for his own
Nor touch it, lest it droop and fall. . . .
Oh, I am not like that at all!

DOROTHY PARKER (1893–1967)

SUNSTRUCK FOXGLOVE

As you bend to touch
The gypsy girl
Who waits for you in the hedge
Her loose dress falls open.

Midsummer ditch-sickness!

Flushed, freckled with earth-fever,
Swollen lips parted, her eyes closing,
A lolling armful, and so young! Hot

Among the insane spiders.
You glimpse the reptile under-speckle
Of her sunburned breasts
And your head swims. You close your eyes.

Can the foxes talk? Your head throbs.
Remember the bird's tolling echo,
The dripping fern-roots, and the butterfly touches
That woke you.

Remember your mother's
Long, dark dugs.

Her silky body a soft oven
For loaves of pollen.

TED HUGHES (1930–98)

IN PRAISE OF ALLIUM

No one celebrates the allium.
The way each purposeful stem
ends in a globe, a domed umbel,
makes people think,
'Drumsticks,' and that's that.
Besides, it's related to the onion.
Is that any reason
for disregard? The flowers – look –

are bouquets of miniature florets,
each with six elfin pointed petals
and some narrower ones my eyes
aren't sharp enough to count,
and three stamens about the size
of a long eyelash.
Every root
sends up a sheaf of sturdy
ridged stems, bounty
to fill your embrace. The bees
care for the allium, if you don't –
hear them now, doing their research,
humming the arias
of a honey opera, Allium it's called,
gold fur voluptuously
brushing that dreamy mauve.

DENISE LEVERTOV (1923–97)

LE SOULCY

I love the lovely violet,
Full dear the pink and pansy hold,
On roses red my heart is set,
But more I love the marigold.

Fair flower in love long since enthralled
By that bright God who shines above;
Unhappy are you rightly called,
Or over-constant in your love?

The God who changed you to a flower
Could never change the will you had:
Tell me if even at this hour
His beauty cannot make you glad?

Ever you lift a languid face
To catch one look as in the past,
And when his light moves from your place
Swiftly your own fades overcast.

I love you, mournful marigold,
I love you, flower of misery,
The more since one tale may be told
Both of our grief and constancy.

I love the lovely violet,
Full dear the pink and pansy hold,
On roses red my heart is set,
But more I love the marigold.

KANGRA FOLK SONG

Flowers blossom in the flower garden,
the pretty woman blossoms
in her own home.

> On the day that you set off for employment,
> locks were put on the palace house, my love.

Locks were put on the palace house,
marigolds withered in the garden, my love.

> Twelve years pass by,
> you never think of me, my love.

I sew men's clothes
and mount a gray horse, my love.

I go forward, where three men sit in a shop
pondering over me, my love.

> 'Shopkeepers sitting around in the shop,
> what discussion are you having?' My love.

> 'One says you're a man,
> another says you're a woman.' My love.

Jumping off the horse, the pretty woman
grabs his arm,
then seats him on the horse.

She spurs the horse, turns it around,
bring him home, my love.

Locks open on the palace house,
marigolds blossom in the garden, my love.

Marigolds blossom in the marigold garden,
the pretty woman blossoms in her own home.

ANON.
TR. KIRIN NARAYAN

MARIGOLDS

Not the flowers men give women –
delicately-scented freesias,
stiff red roses, carnations
the shades of bridesmaids' dresses,
almost sapless flowers,
drying and fading – but flowers
that wilt as soon as their stems
are cut, leaves blackening
as if blighted by the enzymes
in our breath, rotting to a slime
we have to scour from the rims
of vases; flowers that burst
from tight, explosive buds, rayed

135

like the sun, that lit the path
up the Thracian mountain, that we wound
into our hair, stamped on
in ecstatic dance, that remind us
we are killers, can tear the heads
off men's shoulders;
flowers we still bring
secretly and shamefully
into the house, stroking
our arms and breasts and legs
with their hot orange fringes,
the smell of arousal.

VICKI FEAVER (1943–)

LUPINS

They stood. And stood for something. Just by
    standing.
In waiting. Unavailable. But there
For sure. Sure and unbending.
Rose-fingered dawn's and navy midnight's flower.

Seed packets to begin with, pink and azure,
Sifting lightness and small jittery promise:
Lupin spires, erotics of the future,
Lip-brush of the blue and earth's deep purchase.

O pastel turrets, pods and tapering stalks
That stood their ground for all our summer wending
And even when they blanched would never balk.
And none of this surpassed our understanding.

SEAMUS HEANEY (1939–2013)

THRIFT

Born by the sea.
Used to its no-hope moan.
Forty or thereabouts.
Lived on her own.

Heaved a small sigh.
With a handful of stone
to get started,
she saved up the rain.

She came with her cushion
to the cliffs. She sat
strained in the wind
in a pink old-fashioned hat.

No prospect
but the plunge of the beach.
All except nodding,
no speech.

But she worked she worked
to the factory rhythm
of the sea's boredom.
Its bouts of atheism.

And by the weekend
set up a stall
of paper flowers.
And sold them all.

So she made substance out of
lack of substance.
Hard of hearing,
she thrived on silence.

ALICE OSWALD (1966–)

'I WAS THE SLIGHTEST
IN THE HOUSE'

I was the slightest in the house,
I took the smallest room,
At night, my little lamp and book
And one geranium.

So stationed I could catch the mint
That never ceased to fall,

And just my basket, let me think,
I'm sure that this was all.

I never spoke unless addressed,
And then 'twas brief and low,
I could not bear to live aloud
The racket shamed me so.

And if it had not been so far,
And anyone I knew
Were going, I had often thought
How noteless I could die.

EMILY DICKINSON (1830–86)

EVELYN HOPE

Beautiful Evelyn Hope is dead!
  Sit and watch by her side an hour.
That is her book-shelf, this her bed;
  She plucked that piece of geranium-flower,
Beginning to die too, in the glass;
  Little has yet been changed, I think:
The shutters are shut, no light may pass
  Save two long rays thro' the hinge's chink.

Sixteen years old when she died!
  Perhaps she had scarcely heard my name;

It was not her time to love; beside,
  Her life had many a hope and aim,
Duties enough and little cares,
  And now was quiet, now astir,
Till God's hand beckoned unawares, –
  And the sweet white brow is all of her.

Is it too late then, Evelyn Hope?
  What, your soul was pure and true,
The good stars met in your horoscope,
  Made you of spirit, fire and dew –
And, just because I was thrice as old
  And our paths in the world diverged so wide,
Each was nought to each, must I be told?
  We were fellow mortals, nought beside?

No, indeed! for God above
  Is great to grant, as mighty to make,
And creates the love to reward the love:
  I claim you still, for my own love's sake!
Delayed it may be for more lives yet,
  Through worlds I shall traverse, not a few:
Much is to learn, much to forget
  Ere the time be come for taking you.

But the time will come, – at last it will,
  When, Evelyn Hope, what meant (I shall say)
In the lower earth, in the years long still,
  That body and soul so pure and gay?

Why your hair was amber, I shall divine,
    And your mouth of your own geranium's red –
And what you would do with me, in fine,
    In the new life come in the old one's stead.

I have lived (I shall say) so much since then,
    Given up myself so many times,
Gained me the gains of various men,
    Ransacked the ages, spoiled the climes;
Yet one thing, one, in my soul's full scope,
    Either I missed or itself missed me:
And I want and find you, Evelyn Hope!
    What is the issue? let us see!

I loved you, Evelyn, all the while.
    My heart seemed full as it could hold?
There was place and to spare for the frank
        young smile,
    And the red young mouth, and the hair's
        young gold.
So, hush, – I will give you this leaf to keep:
    See, I shut it inside the sweet cold hand!
There, that is our secret: go to sleep!
    You will wake, and remember, and understand.

HOW PANSIES OR HEART'S-EASE CAME FIRST

Frolic virgins once these were,
Over-loving, living here;
Being here their ends denied,
Ran for sweethearts mad, and died.
Love, in pity of their tears,
And their loss in blooming years,
For their restless here-spent hours,
Gave them heart's-ease turn'd to flowers.

ROBERT HERRICK (1591–1674)

A FLOWER-PIECE BY FANTIN

Heart's ease or pansy, pleasure or thought,
Which would the picture give us of these?
Surely the heart that conceived it sought
            Heart's ease.

Surely by glad and divine degrees
The heart impelling the hand that wrought
Wrought comfort here for a soul's disease.

Deep flowers, with lustre and darkness fraught,
From glass that gleams as the chill still seas
Lean and lend for a heart distraught
    Heart's ease.

ALGERNON CHARLES SWINBURNE (1837–1909)

'HEARTSEASE IN MY GARDEN BED'

Heartsease in my garden bed,
    With sweetwilliam white and red,
Honeysuckle on my wall: –
    Heartsease blossoms in my heart
When sweet William comes to call,
    But it withers when we part,
And the honey-trumpets fall.

CHRISTINA ROSSETTI (1830–94)

THE HONEYSUCKLE

I plucked a honeysuckle where
    The hedge on high is quick with thorn,
    And climbing for the prize, was torn,
And fouled my feet in quag-water;

And by the thorns and by the wind
   The blossom that I took was thinn'd,
And yet I found it sweet and fair.

Thence to a richer growth I came,
   Where, nursed in mellow intercourse,
   The honeysuckles sprang by scores,
Not harried like my single stem,
   All virgin lamps of scent and dew.
   So from my hand that first I threw,
Yet plucked not any more of them.

DANTE GABRIEL ROSSETTI (1828–82)

THE WILD HONEY SUCKLE[*]

Fair flower, that dost so comely grow,
Hid in this silent, dull retreat,
Untouched thy honied blossoms blow,
Unseen thy little branches greet:
      No roving foot shall crush thee here,
      No busy hand provoke a tear.

By Nature's self in white arrayed,
She bade thee shun the vulgar eye,
And planted here the guardian shade,
And sent soft waters murmuring by;

Thus quietly thy summer goes,
Thy days declining to repose.

Smit with those charms, that must decay,
I grieve to see your future doom;
They died – nor were those flowers more gay,
The flowers that did in Eden bloom;
    Unpitying frosts, and Autumn's power
    Shall leave no vestige of this flower.

From morning suns and evening dews
At first thy little being came:
If nothing once, you nothing lose,
For when you die you are the same;
    The space between, is but an hour,
    The frail duration of a flower.

PHILIP FRENEAU (1752–1832)

'NOW SLEEPS THE CRIMSON PETAL'
From *The Princess*

Now sleeps the crimson petal, now the white;
Nor waves the cypress in the palace walk;
Nor winks the gold fin in the porphyry font:
The fire-fly wakens: waken thou with me.

Now droops the milkwhite peacock like a ghost,
And like a ghost she glimmers on to me.

Now lies the Earth all Danaë to the stars,
And all thy heart lies open unto me.

Now slides the silent meteor on, and leaves
A shining furrow, as thy thoughts in me.

Now folds the lily all her sweetness up,
And slips into the bosom of the lake:
So fold thyself, my dearest, thou, and slip
Into my bosom and be lost in me.

ALFRED, LORD TENNYSON (1809–92)

THE LILY'S DELUSION

A cold, calm star look'd out of heaven,
    And smiled upon a tranquil lake,
Where, pure as angel's dream at even,
    A Lily lay but half awake.

The flower felt that fatal smile
    And lowlier bow'd her conscious head;
'Why does he gaze on me the while?'
    The light, deluded Lily said.

Poor dreaming flower! – too soon beguiled,
   She cast nor thought nor look elsewhere,
Else she had known the star but smiled
   To see himself reflected there.

FRANCES SARGENT OSGOOD (1811–50)

THE LOTUS

First blooming in the Western Paradise,
The lotus has delighted us for ages.
Its white petals are covered with dew,
Its jade green leaves spread out over the pond,
And its pure fragrance perfumes the wind.
Cool and majestic, it rises from the murky water.
The sun sets behind the mountains
But I remain in the darkness, too captivated to leave.

RYOKAN (1758–1831)   147
TR. JOHN STEVENS

TO THE TUNE OF
'SOARING CLOUDS'

You held my lotus blossom
In your lips and played with the
Pistil. We took one piece of
Magic rhinoceros horn
And could not sleep all night long.
All night the cock's gorgeous crest
Stood erect. All night the bee
Clung trembling to the flower
Stamens. Oh my sweet perfumed
Jewel! I will allow only
My lord to possess my sacred
Lotus pond, and every night
You can make blossom in me
Flowers of fire.

HUANG E (1498–1569)
TR. KENNETH REXROTH

LOTUS BLOSSOM

God knows, we two as a couple
Present a curious sight,
The lady has trouble walking;
Her lover limps outright.

She's like a suffering kitten,
He's as sick as an ailing hound;
As far as heads go, neither
Would seem especially sound.

She is a lotus blossom,
The lady-love thinks in her heart;
He is the moon, so he fancies;
He's pale enough for the part.

The lotus flower is unfurling
By moonlight her little purse,
But in place of life-giving essence
All she gets to conceive is verse.

HEINRICH HEINE (1797–1856)
TR. WALTER ARNDT

THE LOTUS
To M. K. Gandhi

O Mystic Lotus, sacred and sublime,
In myriad-petalled grace inviolate,
Supreme o'er transient storms of tragic Fate,
Deep-rooted in the waters of all Time,
What legions loosed from many a far-off clime
Of wild-bee hordes with lips insatiate,
And hungry winds with wings of hope or hate,

Have thronged and pressed round thy miraculous
    prime
To devastate thy loveliness, to drain
The midmost rapture of thy glorious heart ...
But who could win thy secret, who attain
Thine ageless beauty born of Brahma's breath,
Or pluck thine immortality who art
Coeval with the Lords of Life and Death?

SAROJINI NAIDU (1879–1949)

MAD HONEY SOLILOQUY[5]
[Xenophon, 401 BC]

The soldiers straddled thorn hedges
to sneak a taste. Along the Black Sea,
the honeycombs rose like marmalade jars.
Laurel, scorched oleander, and honey,
that yellow voltage. I tried a drop myself.
Some tasted ambrosia.
Some heard prophetic hymns.
Some cringed at tremors blooming again,
youth in their chests, windshorn Eridanus,
then in the sky, an atomized sun.
And me, I got nothing.

Just another lonesome breeze
freezing my ribs until my muscles
stopped moving. Finally I spat it out.
Like that, my men snapped forward,
purging everything. They purged the honey,
the oleanders, the olives. They purged the suppers
of all the nights they'd ever pined.
They purged the junipers, the stars,
the salt and seaweed. They purged the ocean,
the canker, the long fortnights
spent far away – the Zagros mountains
unlike any hillock back home. Imagine:
a whole field of grown men on all fours.
Armored men in full panoply.
Even through all of this, I fell asleep
half-hoping for a vision, insight, anything.
I would have taken intoxication,
even gagging. As I led these young men
through the waning terrain, the only
prayer I dared was *rid us of our collective needs.*
Socrates once asked me: *If all memories
are theaters, then what can we make
of the shadow scenes, the ones that lurk,
unseen and unexplained?* The question came back
when I saw the dew blind them.
And then at dawn they rose like revenants.

ODES I, 38

PERSICOS ODI, PUER, APPARATUS

Boy! I detest all Persian fopperies;
Fillet-bound garlands are to me disgusting;
Task not thyself with any search, I charge thee,
Where latest roses linger.

Bring me alone (for thou wilt find that readily)
Plain myrtle. Myrtle neither will disparage
Thee occupied to serve me, or me drinking
Beneath my vine's cool shelter.

HORACE (65–8 BC)
TR. WILLIAM COWPER

JEALOUSY

'The Myrtle bush grew shady
Down by the ford.' –
'Is it even so?' said my lady.
'Even so!' said my lord.
'The leaves are set too thick together
For the point of a sword.'

'The arras in your room hangs close,
No light between!
You wedded one of those
That see unseen.' –
'Is it even so?' said the King's Majesty.
'Even so!' said the Queen.

MARY ELIZABETH COLERIDGE (1861–1907)

LEDA

Where the slow river
meets the tide,
a red swan lifts red wings
and darker beak,
and underneath the purple down
of his soft breast
uncurls his coral feet.

Through the deep purple
of the dying heat
of sun and mist,
the level ray of sun-beam
has caressed
the lily with dark breast,
and flecked with richer gold
its golden crest.

Where the slow lifting
of the tide,
floats into the river
and slowly drifts
among the reeds,
and lifts the yellow flags,
he floats
where tide and river meet.

Ah kingly kiss –
no more regret
nor old deep memories
to mar the bliss;
where the low sedge is thick,
the gold day-lily
outspreads and rests
beneath soft fluttering
of red swan wings
and the warm quivering
of the red swan's breast.

THE POET, THE OYSTER,
AND SENSITIVE PLANT

An Oyster, cast upon the shore,
Was heard, though never heard before,
Complaining in a speech well worded,
And worthy thus to be recorded: –
    Ah, hapless wretch! condemn'd to dwell
For ever in my native shell;
Ordain'd to move when others please,
Not for my own content or ease;
But toss'd and buffeted about,
Now *in* the water and now *out*.
'Twere better to be born a stone,
Of ruder shape, and feeling none,
Than with a tenderness like mine,
And sensibilities so fine!
I envy that unfeeling shrub,
Fast rooted against ev'ry rub.
The plant he meant grew not far off,
And felt the sneer with scorn enough:
Was hurt, disgusted, mortified,
And with asperity replied.
    (When, cry the botanists – and stare –
Did plants call'd sensitive grow there?
No matter when – a poet's muse is
To make them grow just where she chooses).

You shapeless nothing in a dish –
You, that are but almost a fish –
I scorn your coarse insinuation,
And have most plentiful occasion
To wish myself the rock I view,
Or such another dolt as you:
For many a grave and learned clerk
And many a gay unletter'd spark,
With curious touch examines me,
If I can feel as well as he;
And, when I bend, retire, and shrink,
Says – Well, 'tis more than one would think!
Thus life is spent (oh fie upon't!)
In being touch'd, and crying – Don't!

A poet, in his ev'ning walk,
O'erheard and check'd this idle talk.
And your fine sense, he said, and yours,
Whatever evil it endures,
Deserves not, if so soon offended,
Much to be pitied or commended.
Disputes, though short, are far too long,
Where both alike are in the wrong;
Your feelings, in their full amount,
Are all upon your own account.

You, in your grotto-work enclos'd,
Complain of being thus expos'd;
Yet nothing feel in that rough coat,

Save when the knife is at your throat,
Wherever driv'n by wind or tide,
Exempt from ev'ry ill beside.

    And as for you, my Lady Squeamish,
Who reckon every touch a blemish,
If all the plants, that can be found
Embellishing the scene around,
Should droop and wither where they grew,
You would not feel at all – not you.
The noblest minds their virtue prove
By pity, sympathy, and love;
These, these are feelings truly fine,
And prove their owner half divine.

    His censure reach'd them as he dealt it,
And each by shrinking show'd he felt it.

WILLIAM COWPER (1731–1829)

HAREBELL

It is not bred by nature
To produce a succulence
With a seed nestling in that.
It is related by name to the Bluebell,
Which has flowers clinging
Like a braid round its fat stem.

The harebell is one flower,
Its solitariness
Bespoke by its colour, not blue
Nor violet; hovering between, precisely.
It is a spare delicate bell.
Inside it are three pale sugary stigmas welded
To each other at equal angles,
Not seen until looked for.
Its stem is thin as wire.
The flower looks down, and if
Lifted, looks fixedly
At the admirer.
Its silence halted between primness and beauty,
Its shape is wrung from the sounds of life round it
As a bell's sound forms the bell's shape from silence,
And resumes its demure integrity;
More precise, more shaped, than the bluebell;
More venturesome. More stirred, ungarrulous.
Stern as a pin.

QUEEN-ANN'S-LACE

Her body is not so white as
anemony petals nor so smooth — nor
so remote a thing. It is a field
of the wild carrot taking
the field by force; the grass
does not raise above it.
Here is no question of whiteness,
white as can be, with a purple mole
at the center of each flower.
Each flower is a hand's span
of her whiteness. Wherever
his hand has lain there is
a tiny purple blemish. Each part
is a blossom under his touch
to which the fibres of her being
stem one by one, each to its end,
until the whole field is a
white desire, empty, a single stem,
a cluster, flower by flower,
a pious wish to whiteness gone over —
or nothing.

WHAT SHE SAID

In the tiny village
on the hillside
where rainclouds play,

the grazing milch cows
remember their young
and return.

In the forest,
the white flowers
of the green-leaved jasmine
redden with the red evening,

and, friend,
I cannot bear it.

VAYILANREVAN (CLASSICAL TAMIL)
TR. A. K. RAMANUJAN

THE FIRST JASMINES

Ah, these jasmines, these white jasmines!
    I seem to remember the first day when I filled my
hands with these jasmines, these white jasmines.
    I have loved the sunlight, the sky and the green
earth;

I have heard the liquid murmur of the river through the darkness of midnight;

Autumn sunsets have come to me at the bend of a road in the lonely waste, like a bride raising her veil to accept her lover.

Yet my memory is still sweet with the first white jasmines that I held in my hands when I was a child.

Many a glad day has come in my life, and I have laughed with merrymakers on festival nights.

On grey mornings of rain I have crooned many an idle song.

I have worn round my neck the evening wreath of *bakulas* woven by the hand of love.

Yet my heart is sweet with the memory of the first fresh jasmines that filled my hands when I was a child.

RABINDRANATH TAGORE (1861–1941)

NIGHT BLOOMING JASMINE

And in the hour when blooms unfurl
thoughts of my loved ones come to me.
    The moths of evening whirl
    around the snowball tree.

Nothing now shouts or sings;
one house only whispers, then hushes.
        Nestlings sleep beneath wings,
        like eyes beneath their lashes.

From open calyces there flows
a ripe strawberry scent, in waves.
        A lamp in the house glows.
        Grasses are born on graves.

A late bee sighs, back from its tours
and no cell vacant any more.
        The hen and her cheeping stars
        cross their threshing floor.

All through the night the flowers flare,
scent flowing and catching the wind.
        The lamp now climbs the stair,
        shines from above, is dimmed ...

It's dawn: the petals, slightly worn,
close up again – each bud to brood,
        in its soft, secret urn,
        on some yet-nameless good.

MY TWO DAUGHTERS

In the cool dusk, enchanting evening drawing on,
One like the dove, the other like the swan,
Lovely, and joyful both of them, and, ah, so sweet,
Big sister and little sister make their seat,
Look, at the threshold of the garden; over them,
A spray of white carnations, long, fragile of stem,
Leans down, immobile, living, over the pair it sees,
Out of an urn of marble, in the sway of the breeze,
And quivers in the shade, and seems at the rim to be
A flight of butterflies suspended in ecstasy.

VICTOR HUGO (1802–85)
TR. PETER DALE SCOTT

FLOWERS OF MIDDLE SUMMER
From *The Winter's Tale*, IV.iv

PERDITA   Sir, the year growing ancient,
    Not yet on summer's death, nor on the birth
    Of trembling winter, the fairest flow'rs o' th'
        season
    Are our carnations, and streaked gillyvors,[6]
    Which some call Nature's bastards; of that kind
    Our rustic garden's barren; and I care not
    To get slips of them.

POLIXENES   Wherefore, gentle maiden,
    Do you neglect them?

PERDITA   For I have heard it said,
    There is an art, which in their piedness shares
    With great creating Nature.

POLIXENES   Say there be;
    Yet Nature is made better by no mean
    But Nature makes that mean; so over that art,
    Which you say adds to Nature, is an art,
    That Nature makes. You see, sweet maid,
                we marry
    A gentler scion to the wildest stock,
    And make conceive a bark of baser kind
    By bud of nobler race. This is an art
    Which does mend Nature, change it rather; but
    The art itself is Nature.

PERDITA   So it is.

POLIXENES Then make your garden rich in gillyvors,
    And do not call them bastards.

PERDITA   I'll not put
    The dibble in earth, to set one slip of them;
    No more than were I painted, I would wish
    This youth should say 'twere well, and only
                therefore
    Desire to breed by me. Here's flow'rs for you:

Hot lavender, mints, savory, marjoram,
The marigold that goes to bed wi' th' sun,
And with him rises, weeping; these are flow'rs
Of middle summer, and I think they are given
To men of middle age. You're very welcome.

WILLIAM SHAKESPEARE (1564–1616)

RED CARNATIONS

If only I could say let's meet at St Pancras,
not below the android-looking couple, clinching
under the clock, but next to Betjeman's statue,
crumpled, loveable, human.

You haven't seen the station, done up
in all its magnificence, the long glitzy
champagne and oyster bar at the track's edge.
I still don't like oysters and you never tried them.

The first thing I'd do is tell about the children:
daughter as good as her word
never working for big business, our son
becoming an arts writer. I know it will never

happen, but if it did, I'd carry a whole bunch
of red carnations, so you couldn't miss me.

PETER PHILLIPS   165

OPIUM POPPIES
From *Metamorphoses*, Book XI

Near the Cimmerians' land a cavern lies
Deep in the hollow of a mountainside,
The home and sanctuary of lazy Sleep,
Where the sun's beams can never reach at morn
Or noon or eve, but cloudy vapours rise
In doubtful twilight ...
There silence dwells: only the lazy stream
Of Lethe 'neath the rock with whisper low
O'er pebbly shallows trickling lulls to sleep.
Before the cavern's mouth lush poppies grow
And countless herbs, from whose bland essences
A drowsy infusion dewy night distils
And sprinkles sleep across the darkening world.

OVID (43 BC–*c.* AD 17)
TR. A. D. MELVILLE

A THING OF BEAUTY

What motley shows are those that bind
    The heavens with yonder height,
Through mists of morning ill defined,
    That half defeat the sight?

Are they the Vizier's tents displayed,
  Where his loved women bide?
Are they the festal carpets laid
  For one most dear – his bride?

Scarlet and white, mixed, freckled, streaked –
  Vision of perfect worth!
Hafiz, how comes thy Shiraz thus
  To greet the cloudy North?

Yes, neighbour popples spreading far,
  A cordial, various band,
As if to scorn the god of war,
  Kindly they robe the land.

So let the sage who serves our earth
  With flowers still make it gay,
And, as this morn, the sun shine forth
  To light them on my way.

[1814]

J. W. VON GOETHE (1749–1832)   167
TR. EDWARD DOWDEN

THE DEATH OF EURYALUS
From *Aeneid*, Book IX

            ... 'Draw on me
your swords, Rutulians! The whole stratagem
was mine, mine only, and the lad ye slay
dared not, and could not. O, by Heaven above
and by the all-beholding stars I swear,
he did but love his hapless friend too well.'
But while he spoke, the furious-thrusting sword
had pierced the tender body, and run through
the bosom white as snow. Euryalus
sank prone in death; upon his goodly limbs
the life-blood ran unstopped, and low inclined
the drooping head; as when some purpled flower,
cut by the ploughshare, dies, or poppies proud
with stem forlorn their ruined beauty bow
before the pelting storm. Then Nisus flew
straight at his foes ...

168 VIRGIL (70–19 BC)
TR. THEODORE C. WILLIAMS

LOVE IN DREAMS

Love hath its poppy-wreath,
    Not Night alone.
I laid my head beneath
    Love's lilied throne:
Then to my sleep he brought
    This anodyne —
The flower of many a thought
    And fancy fine:
A form, a face, no more;
    Fairer than truth;
A dream from death's pale shore;
    The soul of youth:
A dream so dear, so deep,
    All dreams above,
That still I pray to sleep —
    Bring Love back, Love!

THE ÆSTHETE
From *Patience*

If you're anxious for to shine in the high æsthetic line,
    as a man of culture rare,
You must get up all the germs of the transcendental
    terms, and plant them everywhere.
You must lie upon the daisies and discourse in novel
    phrases of your complicated state of mind
(The meaning doesn't matter if it's only idle chatter of
    a transcendental kind).
            And every one will say,
            As you walk your mystic way,
'If this young man expresses himself in terms too deep
    for *me*,
Why, what a very singularly deep young man this
    deep young man must be!'

Be eloquent in praise of the very dull old days which
    have long since passed away,
And convince 'em, if you can, that the reign of good
    QUEEN ANNE was Culture's palmiest day.
Of course you will pooh-pooh whatever's fresh and
    new, and declare it's crude and mean,
And that Art stopped short in the cultivated court of
    the EMPRESS JOSEPHINE.
            And every one will say,
            As you walk your mystic way,

'If that's not good enough for him which is good
     enough for *me*,
Why, what a very cultivated kind of youth this kind of
     youth must be!'

Then a sentimental passion of a vegetable fashion
     must excite your languid spleen,
An attachment *à la* Plato for a bashful young potato,
     or a not-too-French French bean.
Though the Philistines may jostle, you will rank as an
     apostle in the high æsthetic band,
If you walk down Piccadilly with a poppy or a lily in
     your mediæval hand.
          And every one will say,
          As you walk your flowery way,
'If he's content with a vegetable love which would
     certainly not suit *me*,
Why, what a most particularly pure young man this
     pure young man must be!'

W. S. GILBERT (1836–1911)

BREAK OF DAY IN THE TRENCHES

The darkness crumbles away –
It is the same old druid Time as ever.
Only a live thing leaps my hand –

171

A queer sardonic rat –
As I pull the parapet's poppy
To stick behind my ear.
Droll rat, they would shoot you if they knew
Your cosmopolitan sympathies
(And God knows what antipathies).
Now you have touched this English hand
You will do the same to a German –
Soon, no doubt, if it be your pleasure
To cross the sleeping green between.
It seems you inwardly grin as you pass
Strong eyes, fine limbs, haughty athletes
Less chanced than you for life,
Bonds to the whims of murder,
Sprawled in the bowels of the earth,
The torn fields of France.
What do you see in our eyes
At the shrieking iron and flame
Hurled through still heavens?
What quaver – what heart aghast?
Poppies whose roots are in man's veins
Drop, and are ever dropping:
But mine in my ear is safe,
Just a little white with the dust.

POPPIES

The poppies send up their
orange flares; swaying
in the wind, their congregations
are a levitation

of bright dust, of thin
and lacy leaves.
There isn't a place
in this world that doesn't

sooner or later drown
in the indigos of darkness,
but now, for a while,
the roughage

shines like a miracle
as it floats above everything
with its yellow hair.
Of course nothing stops the cold,

black, curved blade
from hooking forward –
of course
loss is the great lesson.

But I also say this: that light
is an invitation
to happiness,
and that happiness,

when it's done right,
is a kind of holiness,
palpable and redemptive.
Inside the bright fields,

touched by their rough and spongy gold,
I am washed and washed
in the river
of earthly delight –

and what are you going to do –
what can you do
about it –
deep, blue night?

AUTUMN

Autumn wind rises: white clouds fly.
Grass and trees wither: geese go south.
Orchids all in bloom: chrysanthemums smell sweet.
I think of my lovely lady: I can never forget.
Floating-pagoda boat crosses Fen River.
Across the mid-stream white waves rise.
Flute and drum keep time to sound of the rower's song;
Amidst revel and feasting, sad thoughts come;
Youth's years how few! Age how sure!

EMPEROR WU-TI (157–87 BC)
TR. ARTHUR WALEY

SUNFLOWER

Its radiance bursts forth in summer's bright light,
In clusters nestling along the dense green shade.
Evenings, it droops like the common hibiscus,
But blazes at noon with the pomegranate flowers.
A subtle scent spreads across our mat,
A fresh splendor shines upon our feast.
When all the other flowers have bid us farewell,
This last survivor now rouses our pity.

KAO CH'I (1336–74)
TR. IRVING Y. LO

'AH! SUN-FLOWER'

Ah Sun-flower! weary of time,
Who countest the steps of the Sun,
Seeking after that sweet golden clime
Where the traveller's journey is done:

Where the Youth pined away with desire,
And the pale Virgin shrouded in snow,
Arise from their graves and aspire
Where my Sun-flower wishes to go.

WILLIAM BLAKE (1757–1827)

YELLOW SUNFLOWER OF SZECHWAN

Rare flower, leaf-fringed, of tender yellow gold –
Its sheen, reflected on my studio window, penetrates
    the bamboo grove.
What could prevent a beautiful girl from casually
    smelling it?
I almost thought it was her lover's mouth imprinted
    in the center.

CHANG YU (*fl.* 810)
TR. IRVING Y. LO

THE SUNFLOWER

Bring me the sunflower here and let me set it
in the parched briny soil of my own place
to turn all day to the heavens that reflect it
the broad gaze of its yellow yearning face.

Things of the dark aspire to all that's bright,
their forms dissolving into a cascade
of tints merging in music. Simply to fade
from view is the great adventure, lost in light.

Bring me the plant that points us to the height
where there's a clearness tinged with the sun's rays
and life itself is thinning to a haze.
Bring me that flower delirious with light.

EUGENIO MONTALE (1896–1981)
TR. PATRICIA HANN

THE RAGWORT

Ragwort, thou humble flower with tattered leaves
I love to see thee come & litter gold,
What time the summer binds her russet sheaves;
Decking rude spots in beautys manifold
That without thee were dreary to behold
Sun burnt & bare – the meadow bank the baulk
That leads a waggonway through mellow fields
Rich with the tints that harvests plenty yields
Browns of all hues – & every where I walk
Thy waste of shining blossoms richly shields
The sun tanned sward in splendid hues that burn
So bright & glaring that the very light
Of the rich sunshine doth to paleness turn
& seems but very shadows in thy sight.

JOHN CLARE (1793–1864)   179

RAGWORT

They won't let railways alone, these ragged flowers.
They're some remorseless joy of dereliction
darkest banks exhale like vivid breath
as bricks divide to let them root between.
How every falling place concocts their smile,
taking what's left and making a song of it.

ANNE STEVENSON (1933–)

AUTUMN CROCUSES

In fall the fields are poisonous but fair
Where, slowly poisoning, the cattle graze.
The meadow saffron, *colchicum*, thrives there,
Color of lilac and the circles under eyes.
My life pastures so on the autumn hue
Of your eyes and slowly poisons itself too.
Children in queer jackets come and play
Harmonicas and pick the purple flowers
Which are like mothers, their own daughters'
    daughters.
When your saffron eyelids raise and lower
They are like flowers that a crazy wind flutters.

The shepherd sings the cattle on their way
As, slow and lowingly and for all time, they pass
From the broad evil-flowered autumn grass.

GUILLAUME APOLLINAIRE (1880–1918)
TR. WILLIAM MEREDITH

AUTUMN

They brought me a quilled, yellow dahlia,
Opulent, flaunting.
Round gold
Flung out of a pale green stalk.
Round, ripe gold
Of maturity,
Meticulously frilled and flaming,
A fire-ball of proclamation:
Fecundity decked in staring yellow
For all the world to see.
They brought a quilled, yellow dahlia,
To me who am barren.
Shall I send it to you,
You who have taken with you
All I once possessed?

AMY LOWELL (1874–1925)

A DAHLIA

Hard-bosomed courtesan, magnificent
Marble-glossed figure; eye opaque, of solid
Brown, opening like a bull's, languid and stolid.

Flower ornate and richly plump; no scent
Wafts round you, and your body's graceful ease
Rolls free – then mutes – its flawless harmonies.

Yours is not even flesh's scent, that those
Hay-tossing belles exude; rather, you pose
Idol unmoved by incense burned before you.

– Such is the Dahlia, king nobly costumed:
You hold your head high, modest, unperfumed,
Irksome, among the jasmines, who abhor you!

THE SMALLER ORCHID

Love is a climate
small things find safe
to grow in – not
(though I once supposed so)
the demanding cattleya
du côté de chez Swann,
glamor among the faubourgs,
hothouse overpowerings, blisses
and cruelties at teatime, but this
next-to-unidentifiable wildling,
hardly more than a
sprout, I've found
flourishing in the hollows
of a granite seashore –
a cheerful tousle, little,
white, down-to-earth orchid
declaring its authenticity,
if you hug the ground
close enough, in a powerful
outdoorsy-domestic
whiff of vanilla.

I descended to the valley to gather orchids
But the basin was blanketed with frost and dew,
And it took all day to find the flowers.
Suddenly I thought of an old friend
Separated from me by miles of mountains and
    rivers.
Will we ever meet again?
I gaze toward the sky,
Tears streaming down my cheeks.

RYOKAN (1758–1831)
TR. JOHN STEVENS

CARNATIONS

Pale blossoms, each balanced on a single jointed stem,
And leaves curled back in elaborate Corinthian scrolls;
And the air cool, as if drifting down from wet
    hemlocks,
Or rising out of ferns not far from water,
A crisp hyacinthine coolness,
Like that clear autumnal weather of eternity,
The windless perpetual morning above a September
    cloud.

184 THEODORE ROETHKE (1908–63)

SHELTERED GARDEN

I have had enough.
I gasp for breath.

Every way ends, every road,
every foot-path leads at last
to the hill-crest –
then you retrace your steps,
or find the same slope on the other side,
precipitate.

I have had enough –
border-pinks, clove-pinks, wax-lilies,
herbs, sweet-cress.

O for some sharp swish of a branch –
there is no scent of resin
in this place,
no taste of bark, of coarse weeds,
aromatic, astringent –
only border on border of scented pinks.

Have you seen fruit under cover
that wanted light –
pears wadded in cloth,
protected from the frost,
melons, almost ripe,
smothered in straw?

Why not let the pears cling
to the empty branch?
All your coaxing will only make
a bitter fruit –
let them cling, ripen of themselves,
test their own worth,
nipped, shrivelled by the frost,
to fall at last but fair
with a russet coat.

Or the melon –
let it bleach yellow
in the winter light,
even tart to the taste –
it is better to taste of frost –
the exquisite frost –
than of wadding and of dead grass.

For this beauty,
beauty without strength,
chokes out life.
I want wind to break,
scatter these pink-stalks,
snap off their spiced heads,
fling them about with dead leaves –
spread the paths with twigs,
limbs broken off,
trail great pine branches,

hurled from some far wood
right across the melon-patch,
break pear and quince –
leave half-trees, torn, twisted
but showing the fight was valiant.

O to blot out this garden
to forget, to find a new beauty
in some terrible
wind-tortured place.

H. D. (HILDA DOOLITTLE) (1886–1961)

HIGH WAVING HEATHER

High waving heather 'neath stormy blasts bending
Midnight and moonlight and bright shining stars
Darkness and glory rejoicingly blending
Earth rising to heaven and heaven descending
Man's spirit away from its drear dungeon sending
Bursting the fetters and breaking the bars

All down the mountain sides wild forests lending
One mighty voice to the life giving wind
Rivers their banks in the jubilee rending
Fast through the valleys a reckless course wending
Wider and deeper their waters extending
Leaving a desolate desert behind

Shining and lowering and swelling and dying
Changing forever from midnight to noon
Roaring like thunder like soft music sighing
Shadows on shadows advancing and flying
Lightning bright flashes the deep gloom defying
Coming as swiftly and fading as soon

EMILY BRONTË (1818–48)

BAVARIAN GENTIANS

Not every man has gentians in his house
in Soft September, at slow, Sad Michaelmas.

Bavarian gentians, big and dark, only dark
darkening the daytime, torch-like with the smoking
    blueness of Pluto's gloom,
ribbed and torch-like, with their blaze of darkness
    spread blue
down flattening into points, flattened under the sweep
    of white day
torch-flower of the blue-smoking darkness, Pluto's
    dark-blue daze,
black lamps from the halls of Dis, burning dark blue,
giving off darkness, blue darkness, as Demeter's pale
    lamps give off light,
lead me then, lead me the way.

Reach me a gentian, give me a torch!
let me guide myself with the blue, forked torch of this
    flower
down the darker and darker stairs, where blue is
    darkened on blueness,
even where Persephone goes, just now, from the
    frosted September
to the sightless realm where darkness is awake upon
    the dark
and Persephone herself is but a voice
or a darkness invisible enfolded in the deeper dark
of the arms Plutonic, and pierced with the passion of
    dense gloom,
among the splendour of torches of darkness, shedding
    darkness on the lost bride and her groom.

D. H. LAWRENCE (1885–1930)

TO THE FRINGED GENTIAN

Thou blossom bright with autumn dew,
And colored with the heaven's own blue,
That openest when the quiet light
Succeeds the keen and frosty night,

Thou comest not when violets lean
O'er wandering brooks and springs unseen,

Or columbines, in purple dressed,
Nod o'er the ground-bird's hidden nest.

Thou waitest late and com'st alone,
When woods are bare and birds are flown,
And frost and shortening days portend
The aged year is near his end.

Then doth thy sweet and quiet eye
Look through its fringes to the sky,
Blue – blue – as if that sky let fall
A flower from its cerulean wall.

I would that thus, when I shall see
The hour of death draw near to me,
Hope, blossoming within my heart,
May look to heaven as I depart.

WILLIAM CULLEN BRYANT (1794–1878)

'THERE IS A FLOWER
THAT BEES PREFER'

There is a flower that bees prefer,
And butterflies desire;
To gain the purple democrat
The humming-birds aspire.

And whatsoever insect pass,
A honey bears away
Proportioned to his several dearth
And her capacity.

Her face is rounder than the moon,
And ruddier than the gown
Of orchis in the pasture,
Or rhododendron worn.

She doth not wait for June;
Before the world is green
Her sturdy little countenance
Against the wind is seen,

Contending with the grass,
Near kinsman to herself,
For privilege of sod and sun,
Sweet litigants for life.

And when the hills are full,
And newer fashions blow,
Doth not retract a single spice
For pang of jealousy.

Her public is the noon,
Her providence the sun,
Her progress by the bee proclaimed
In sovereign, swerveless tune.

The bravest of the host,
Surrendering the last,
Nor even of defeat aware
When cancelled by the frost.[7]

EMILY DICKINSON (1830–86)

Three Michaelmas daisies
on an ashtray;
one abets love;
one droops and woos;

one stiffens her petals
remembering
the root, the sap
and the bees' play.

BASIL BUNTING (1900–85)

WILD ASTERS

In the spring I asked the daisies
If his words were true,
And the clever, clear-eyed daisies
Always knew.

Now the fields are brown and barren,
Bitter autumn blows,
And of all the stupid asters
Not one knows.

SARA TEASDALE (1884–1933)

STAR-WORT
From *Georgics*, IV

There is a useful flower
Growing in the meadows, which the country folk
Call star-wort, not a blossom hard to find,
For its large cluster lifts itself in air
Out of one root; its central orb is gold
But it wears petals in a numerous ring
Of glossy purplish blue; 'tis often laid
In twisted garlands at some holy shrine.
Bitter its taste; the shepherds gather it
In valley-pastures where the winding streams
Of Mella flow. The roots of this steeped well
In hot, high-flavored wine, thou may'st set down
At the hive door in baskets heaping full.

TRANSLATED BY THEODORE C. WILLIAMS

THE FIELD PANSY

Yesterday, just before the first frost of the season,
I discovered a violet in bloom on the lawn – a white one,
with a mesh of faint purple pencil marks above the
    hollow
at the throat, where the petals join: an irregular, a waif,
out of sync with the ubiquity of the asters of New
    England,

or indeed with the johnny-jump-ups I stopped to
    look at,
last week, in a plot by the sidewalk: weedily prolific
common garden perennial whose lineage goes back to
the bi- or tri-colored native field pansy of Europe:
ancestor of the cloned ocher and aubergine, the cream-
    white,

the masked motley, the immaculate lilac-blue of the
    pansies
that thrive in the tended winter plots of tidewater
    Virginia,
where in spring the cutover fields at the timber's edge,
away from the boxwood and magnolia alleys, are
    populous
with an indigenous, white, just faintly suffused-with-
    violet

first cousin: a link with what, among the hollows
        of the
great dunes of Holland, out of reach of the slide
        and hurl
of the North Sea breakers, I found growing a summer
        ago – a
field pansy tinged not violet but pink, sometimes
        approaching
the hue of the bell of a foxglove: a gathering, a
        proliferation

on a scale that, for all its unobtrusiveness, seems to be
worldwide, of what I don't know how to read except
        as an
urge to give pleasure: a scale that may, for all our
        fazed
dubiety, indeed be universal. I know I'm leaving
        something out
when I write of this omnipresence of something like
        eagerness,

this gushing insouciance that appears at the same time
        capable
of an all but infinite particularity: sedulous, patient,
        though
in the end (so far as anyone can see) without
        consequence.

What is consequence? What difference do the
        minutiae
of that seeming inconsequence that's called beauty

add up to? Life was hard in the hinterland, where
        spring arrived
with a gush of violets, sky-blue out of the ground of
        the woodlot,
but where a woman was praised by others of her sex
        for being
Practical, and by men not at all, other than in a slow
        reddening
about the neck, a callowly surreptitious wolf-whistle:
        where the mode

was stoic, and embarrassment stood in the way of
        affect:
a mother having been alarmingly seen in tears,
        once only
we brought her a fistful of johnny-jump-ups from
        the garden,
'because you were crying' – and saw we'd done the
        wrong thing.

POPPIES IN OCTOBER
for Helder and Suzette Macedo

Even the sun-clouds this morning cannot manage
        such skirts.
Nor the woman in the ambulance
Whose red heart blooms through her coat so
        astoundingly –

A gift, a love gift
Utterly unasked for
By a sky

Palely and flamily
Igniting its carbon monoxides, by eyes
Dulled to a halt under bowlers.

O my God, what am I
That these late mouths should cry open
In a forest of frost, in a dawn of cornflowers.

SICILIAN CYCLAMENS

When he pushed his bush of black hair off his brow:
When she lifted her mop from her eyes, and screwed it
    in a knob behind
        – O act of fearful temerity!
When they felt their foreheads bare, naked to heaven,
    their eyes revealed:
When they felt the light of heaven brandished like a
    knife at their defenceless eyes,
And the sea like a blade at their face,
Mediterranean savages:
When they came out, face-revealed, under heaven,
    from the shaggy undergrowth of their own hair
For the first time,
They saw tiny rose cyclamens between their toes,
    growing
Where the slow toads sat brooding on the past.

Slow toads, and cyclamen leaves
Stickily glistening with eternal shadow
Keeping to earth.
Cyclamen leaves
Toad-filmy, earth-iridescent
Beautiful
Frost-filigreed
Spumed with mud

Snail-nacreous
Low down.

The shaking aspect of the sea
And man's defenceless bare face
And cyclamens putting their ears back.

Long, pensive, slim-muzzled greyhound buds
Dreamy, not yet present,
Drawn out of earth
At his toes.

Dawn-rose
Sub-delighted, stone-engendered
Cyclamens, young cyclamens
Arching
Waking, pricking their ears
Like delicate very-young greyhound bitches
Half-yawning at the open, inexperienced
Vista of day,
Folding back their soundless petalled ears.

Greyhound bitches
Bending their rosy muzzles pensive down,
And breathing soft, unwilling to wake to the new day
Yet sub-delighted.

Ah Mediterranean morning, when our world began!
Far-off Mediterranean mornings,

Pelasgic faces uncovered,
And unbudding cyclamens.

The hare suddenly goes uphill
Laying back her long ears with unwinking bliss.

And up the pallid, sea-blenched Mediterranean
    stone-slopes
Rose cyclamen, ecstatic fore-runner!
Cyclamens, ruddy-muzzled cyclamens
In little bunches like bunches of wild hares
Muzzles together, ears a-prick,
Whispering witchcraft
Like women at a well, the dawn-fountain.

Greece, and the world's morning
Where all the Parthenon marbles still fostered the
    roots of the cyclamen.
Violets
Pagan, rosy-muzzled violets
Autumnal
Dawn-pink,
Dawn-pale
Among squat toad-leaves sprinkling the unborn
Erechtheion marbles.

THE CHRYSANTHEMUMS IN
THE EASTERN GARDEN

The days of my youth left me long ago;
And now in their turn dwindle my years of prime.
With what thoughts of sadness and loneliness
I walk again in this cold, deserted place!
In the midst of the garden long I stand alone;
The sunshine, faint; the wind and dew chill.
The autumn lettuce is tangled and turned to seed;
The fair trees are blighted and withered away.
All that is left are a few chrysanthemum-flowers
That have newly opened beneath the wattled fence.
I had brought wine and meant to fill my cup,
When the sight of these made me stay my hand.

               I remember, when I was young,
How quickly my mood changed from sad to gay.
If I saw wine, no matter at what season,
Before I drank it, my heart was already glad.

                    But now that age comes
A moment of joy is harder and harder to get.
And always I fear that when I am quite old
The strongest liquor will leave me comfortless.
Therefore I ask you, late chrysanthemum-flower,
At this late season why do you bloom alone?
Though well I know that it was not for my sake,
Taught by you, for a while I will smooth my frown.

PO CHU-I (772–846)   201
TR. ARTHUR WALEY

CROWNED WITH DREAMS

That was the day of the white chrysanthemums –
Its brilliance almost frightened me . . .
And then, then you came to take my soul
at the dead of night.

I was so frightened, and you came sweetly and gently,
I had been thinking of you in my dreams.
You came, and soft as a fairy tune
the night rang out . . .

RAINER MARIA RILKE (1875–1926)
TR. RICHARD STOKES

   They spoke no word,
The host, the guest,
      And the white chrysanthemum.

RYOTA (1718–87)
TR. R. H. BLYTH

WINTER

On the oak table, earth-islanded in their bowl,
Or stilled, a fountain, in their vase, they tell our year's
    mid-night
And turn our thoughts to east with scent and cold of dawn.

E. J. SCOVELL
MID-WINTER FLOWERS

STAR OF BETHLEHEM[8]

We called it that when we were very young,
before we'd learned about epiphanies
through Father's crackly 78, sung
by Richard Crooks, the school nativities,
the 'sorrowing, sighing, bleeding
dying' of our Colleen Bawn carol choir –
beer-soaked bass, and baritone receding,
sopranos launched by Aunty Nola's higher
than hyena halleluia – all these
were pretty damn close to epiphanies.

My mother banned it from the flower beds;
to her it ranked with stinkblaar as a chronic
garden weed: the glossy leaves, the flat heads
in white and purple, smelling of tonic,
she did not hesitate to destroy. She
called them 'missionary plants', the housewives'
bane. Yet these flowers of nativity
which, healers claim, are saving many lives:
curing cancer and Hodgkin's disease,
are pretty close to epiphanies.

It took one long day to dig that bunker.
I broke the handle of my spade. The ground
was rock hard. Nothing grew there but paper
thorns and, wonderfully: five petals, round

and white and smelling of tonic, opened flat
against the sky: a Star of Bethlehem.
I picked it and stuffed it in my combat
jacket on top of a phosphorous bomb.
I want to tell you: moments such as these
are pretty damn close to epiphanies.

JOHN EPPEL (1947–)

THE ORCHID HOUSE

A flower's fragrance is a woman's virtue;
So I tell them underground in pairs,
Or in their fleshy white sleeves, how
Desirable their shapes, how one
Was lost for sixty years, with all
Its arching spikes, its honeyed tessellations,
And how in bloom they will resemble
Moths, the gloss of mirrors, Christmas
Stars, their helmets blushing
Red-brown when they marry.

IN A CUBAN GARDEN

Hibiscus flowers are cups of fire,
    (Love me, my lover, life will not stay)
The bright poinsettia shakes in the wind,
    A scarlet leaf is blowing away.

A lizard lifts his head and listens –
    Kiss me before the noon goes by,
Here in the shade of the ceiba hide me
    From the great black vulture circling the sky.

SARA TEASDALE (1884–1933)

'IN MY SMALL GARDEN'

I
In my small garden
the modest daisy blooms,
so abundant and humble –
yet artless and simple.

She weaves rich embroideries in the grass
    and creates wonders
amidst cool, verdant meadows
where oaks cast their shadows,
along the banks of the spring
and in the shade of the silent brook.

And even when trampled,
she recovers, rises again
unsullied, like white souls
that envy tries in vain to blacken.

II

When December brings abundant rain,
like acacias, the daisies blossom
with the same pure fragrance
of those I once fervently adored.

How very foolish are my memories,
since I buried them with my own hand!
Those pale leaves are not the ones I kissed,
nor am I the same I once was.

ROSALÍA DE CASTRO (1837–85)
TR. ANNA-MARIA ALDAZ, BARBARA N. GANTT
AND ANNE C. BROMLEY

'THE BLUE BELL IS
THE SWEETEST FLOWER'[9]

The blue bell is the sweetest flower
That waves in summer air
Its blossoms have the mightiest power
To soothe my spirit's care

There is a spell in purple heath
Too wildly, sadly drear
The violet has a fragrant breath
But fragrance will not cheer

The trees are bare, the sun is cold
And seldom, seldom seen –
The heavens have lost their zone of gold
The earth its robe of green

And ice upon the glancing stream
Has cast its sombre shade
And distant hills and valleys seem
In frozen mist arrayed –

The blue bell cannot charm me now
The heath has lost its bloom
The violets in the glen below
They yield no sweet perfume

But though I mourn the heather-bell
'Tis better far, away
I know how fast my tears would swell
To see it smile today

And that wood flower that hides so shy
Beneath the mossy stone
Its balmy scent and dewy eye
'Tis not for them I moan

It is the slight and stately stem
The blossom's silvery blue
The buds hid like a sapphire gem
In sheaths of emerald hue

'Tis these that breathe upon my heart
A calm and softening spell
That if it makes the tear-drop start
Has power to soothe as well

For these I weep, so long divided
Through winter's dreary day
In longing weep – but most when guided
On withered banks to stray

If chilly then the light should fall
Adown the dreary sky
And gild the dank and darkened wall
With transient brilliancy

How do I yearn, how do I pine
For the time of flowers to come
And turn me from that fading shine
To mourn the fields of home –

ROSEMARY

Beauty and Beauty's son and rosemary –
Venus and Love, her son, to speak plainly –
born of the sea supposedly,
at Christmas each, in company,
braids a garland of festivity.
    Not always rosemary –

since the flight to Egypt, blooming differently.
With lancelike leaf, green but silver underneath,
its flowers – white originally –
turned blue. The herb of memory,
imitating the blue robe of Mary,
    is not too legendary

to flower both as symbol and as pungency.
Springing from stones beside the sea,
the height of Christ when thirty-three,
it feeds on dew and to the bee
'hath a dumb language'; is in reality
    a kind of Christmas tree.

'GREEN GROWETH THE HOLLY'

Green groweth the holly, so doth the ivy.
Though winter blasts blow never so high,
Green groweth the holly.

As the holly groweth green
   And never changeth hue,
So I am, and ever hath been,
    Unto my lady true.
      Green groweth ... etc.

As the holly groweth green,
   With ivy all alone,
When flowerys cannot be seen
   And green-wood leaves be gone,
    ut supra

Now unto my lady
   Promise to her I make:
From all other only
   To her I me betake.
    ut supra

Adieu, mine own lady,
   Adieu, my specïal,
Who hath my heart truly,
   Be sure, and ever shall.

Green groweth the holly, so doth the ivy.
Though winter blasts blow never so high,
Green groweth the holly.

KING HENRY VIII (ATTRIB.) (1491–1547)

Winter wind –
camellia blossoms have fixed
their make-up

ISSA (1763–1828)
TR. DAVID G. LANOUE

THE CAMELLIA
From Balzac's *Les Illusions perdus*

In Nature's poem flowers have each their word:
The rose of love and beauty sings alone;
The violet's soul exhales in tenderest tone;
The lily's one pure simple note is heard.
The cold Camellia only, stiff and white,
Rose without perfume, lily without grace,
When chilling winter shows his icy face,
Blooms for a world that vainly seeks delight.
Yet, in a theatre, or ball-room light,

With alabaster petals opening fair,
I gladly see Camellias shining bright
Above some stately woman's raven hair,
Whose noble form fulfils the heart's desire,
Like Grecian marbles warmed by Phidian fire.

CHARLES LASSAILLY (1806–43)
TR. KATHARINE PRESCOTT WORMELEY

CYCLAMENS

They are terribly white:
　　There is snow on the ground,
And a moon on the snow at night;
The sky is cut by the winter light;
Yet I, who have all these things in ken,
Am struck to the heart by the chiselled white
　　Of this handful of cyclamen.

MICHAEL FIELD (KATHERINE BRADLEY, 1846–1914,
AND EDITH COOPER, 1862–1913)

narcissus –
 and the white paper screen,
  reflecting each other

its color
 whiter than the peach:
  narcissus bloom

BASHO (1644–94)
TR. DAVID LANDIS BARNHILL

ODE TO THE SNOW-DROP

The Snow-drop, Winter's timid child,
  Awakes to life, bedew'd with tears;
And flings around its fragrance mild;
And where no rival flow'rets bloom,
Amid the bare and chilling gloom,
  A beauteous gem appears!

All weak and wan, with head inclin'd,
    Its parent-breast the drifted snow;
It trembles, while the ruthless wind
Bends its slim form; the tempest lowers,
Its em'rald eye drops crystal show'rs
    On its cold bed below.

Poor flow'r! on thee the sunny beam
    No touch of genial warmth bestows;
Except to thaw the icy stream
    Whose little current purls along,
And whelms thee as it flows.

The night-breeze tears thy silky dress,
    Which deck'd with silvery lustre shone;
The morn returns, not thee to bless. –
    The gaudy *Crocus* flaunts its pride,
    And triumphs where its rival – died
    Unshelter'd and unknown!

No sunny beam shall gild thy grave,
    No bird of pity thee deplore:
There shall no verdant branches wave,
        For spring shall all her gems unfold,
        And revel 'midst her beds of gold,
    When thou art seen no more!

Where'er I find thee, gentle flow'r,
    Thou still art sweet, and dear to me!
For I have known the cheerless hour,
    Have seen the sun-beams cold and pale,
    Have felt the chilling, wint'ry gale,
And wept, and shrunk like thee!

<small>MARY ROBINSON</small> (1758–1800)

SNOWDROP

Now is the globe shrunk tight
Round the mouse's dulled wintering heart.
Weasel and crow, as if moulded in brass,
Move through an outer darkness
Not in their right minds,
With the other deaths. She, too, pursues her ends,
Brutal as the stars of this month,
Her pale head heavy as metal.

<small>TED HUGHES</small> (1930–98)   217

ENDURE HARDNESS

A cold wind stirs the blackthorn
   To burgeon and to blow,
Besprinkling half-green hedges
   With flakes and sprays of snow.

Through coldness and through keenness,
   Dear hearts, take comfort so:
Somewhere or other doubtless
   These make the blackthorn blow.

CHRISTINA ROSSETTI (1830–94)

THE ORDER OF SAYING

'As soon as the blackthorn comes in flower
   The wind blows cold,' she says:
I see those bushes tossed and whitening,
   Drawing the light and currents of the air
Into their mass and depth; can only see
   The order of her saying in that flare
That rises like a beacon for the wind
   To flow into, to twist and wear
Garment and incandescence, flag of spring.

DEMETER

Where I lived – winter and hard earth.
I sat in my cold stone room
choosing tough words, granite, flint,

to break the ice. My broken heart –
I tried that, but it skimmed,
flat, over the frozen lake.

She came from a long, long way,
but I saw her at last, walking,
my daughter, my girl, across the fields,

in bare feet, bringing all spring's flowers
to her mother's house. I swear
the air softened and warmed as she moved,

the blue sky smiling, none too soon,
with the small shy mouth of a new moon.

THE LANGUAGE
OF FLOWERS

Love's language may be talked with these;
To work out choicest sentences,
   No blossoms can be meeter;
And, such being used in Eastern bowers,
Young maids may wonder if the flowers
   Or meanings be the sweeter.

ELIZABETH BARRET BROWNING
A FLOWER IN A LETTER

Rose is a rose is a rose is a rose.

GERTRUDE STEIN

THE MYRTLE

'Though no word may be spoken,
   My welfare to tell,
When I send thee a token,
   Decypher it well:
In my desolate hours
   My solace shall be,
In the language of flowers
   To whisper to thee.'

He spoke, – and we parted;
   I said not a word;
For, half broken-hearted,
   His farewell I heard;
And when I was lonely,
   Sweet tokens he sent,
For me, and me only,
   To trace their intent.

I watch'd for their coming;
   They came, – but they brought,
Though fragrant and blooming,
   Not tidings I sought!
All told me of sorrow,
   Of absence, of pain!
None whispered, 'To-morrow,
   We meet, Love, again.'

No Flower hath spoken
　　Of hope until now!
How welcome this token,
　　The green Myrtle bough!
No gift could be better;
　　Unless he would write,
Three words in a letter, –
　　'Expect me to-night.'

<small>THOMAS HAYNES BAYLY</small> (1797–1839)

LOVE-LETTERS MADE OF FLOWERS
On a Print of one of them in a Book

An exquisite invention this,
Worthy of Love's most honied kiss,
This art of writing *billet-doux*
In buds, and odours, and bright hues!
In saying all one feels and thinks
In clever daffodils and pinks;
In puns of tulips; and in phrases,
Charming for their truth, of daisies;
Uttering, as well as silence may,
The sweetest words the sweetest way.
How fit too for the lady's bosom!
The place where *billet-doux* repose 'em.

What delight, in some sweet spot
Combining *love* with *garden* plot,
At once to cultivate one's flowers
And one's epistolary powers!
Growing one's own choice words and fancies
In orange tubs, and beds of pansies;
One's sighs and passionate declarations
In odorous rhetoric of carnations;
Seeing how far one's stocks will reach;
Taking due care one's flowers of speech
To guard from blight as well as bathos,
And watering, every day, one's pathos!

A letter comes, just gather'd. We
Dote on its tender brilliancy;
Inhale its delicate expressions
Of balm and pea, and its confessions
Made with as sweet a *Maiden's Blush*
As ever morn bedew'd on bush,
('Tis in reply to one of ours,
Made of the most convincing flowers,)
Then after we have kiss'd its wit
And heart, in water putting it,
(To keep its remarks fresh,) go round
Our little eloquent plot of ground,
And with enchanted hands compose
Our answer all of lily and rose,

Of tuberose and of violet,
And *Little Darling* (Mignonette)
Of *Look at me* and *Call me to you*,
(Words that while they greet, go through you),
Of *Thoughts*, of *Flames*, *Forget-me-not*,
Bridewort, – in short, the whole blest lot
Of vouchers for a life-long kiss,
And literally, breathing bliss.

LEIGH HUNT (1784–1859)

A LETTER OF ADVICE

*From Miss Medora Trevilian, at Padua,
to Miss Araminta Vavasour, in London*

You tell me you're promised a lover,
    My own Araminta, next week;
Why cannot my fancy discover
    The hue of his coat and his cheek?
Alas! if he look like another,
    A vicar, a banker, a beau,
Be deaf to your father and mother,
    My own Araminta, say 'No!'

Miss Lane, at her Temple of Fashion,
    Taught us both how to sing and to speak,
And we loved one another with passion,
    Before we had been there a week:
You gave me a ring for a token;
    I wear it wherever I go;
I gave you a chain, – is it broken?
    My own Araminta, say 'No!'

O think of our favourite cottage,
    And think of our dear Lalla Rookh!
How we shared with the milkmaids their pottage,
    And drank of the stream from the brook;
How fondly our loving lips faltered,
    'What further can grandeur bestow?'
My heart is the same; – is yours altered?
    My own Araminta, say 'No!'

Remember the thrilling romances
    We read on the bank in the glen;
Remember the suitors our fancies
    Would picture for both of us then.
They wore the red cross on their shoulder,
    They had vanquished and pardoned their foe –
Sweet friend, are you wiser or colder?
    My own Araminta, say 'No!'

You know, when Lord Rigmarole's carriage,
  Drove off with your Cousin Justine,
You wept, dearest girl, at the marriage,
  And whispered 'How base she has been!'
You said you were sure it would kill you,
  If ever your husband looked so;
And you will not apostatize, – will you?
  My own Araminta, say 'No!'

When I heard I was going abroad, love,
  I thought I was going to die;
We walked arm in arm to the road, love,
  We looked arm in arm to the sky;
And I said 'When a foreign postilion
  Has hurried me off to the Po,
Forget not Medora Trevilian:
  My own Araminta, say "No"!'

We parted! but sympathy's fetters
  Reach far over valley and hill;
I muse o'er your exquisite letters,
  And feel that your heart is mine still;
And he who would share it with me, love, –
  The richest of treasures below, –
If he's not what Orlando should be, love,
  My own Araminta, say 'No!'

If he wears a top-boot in his wooing,
  If he comes to you riding a cob,
If he talks of his baking or brewing,
  If he puts up his feet on the hob,
If he ever drinks port after dinner,
  If his brow or his breeding is low,
If he calls himself 'Thompson' or 'Skinner,'
  My own Araminta, say 'No!'

If he studies the news in the papers
  While you are preparing the tea,
If he talks of the damps or the vapours
  While moonlight lies soft on the sea,
If he's sleepy while you are capricious,
  If he has not a musical 'Oh!'
If he does not call Werther delicious, –
  My own Araminta, say 'No!'

If he ever sets foot in the City
  Among the stockbrokers and Jews,
If he has not a heart full of pity,
  If he don't stand six feet in his shoes,
If his lips are not redder than roses,
  If his hands are not whiter than snow,
If he has not the model of noses, –
  My own Araminta, say 'No!'

If he speaks of a tax or a duty,
    If he does not look grand on his knees,
If he's blind to a landscape of beauty,
    Hills, valleys, rocks, waters, and trees,
If he dotes not on desolate towers,
    If he likes not to hear the blast blow,
If he knows not the language of flowers, –
    My own Araminta, say 'No!'

He must walk – like a god of old story
    Come down from the home of his rest;
He must smile – like the sun in his glory
    On the buds he loves ever the best;
And oh! from its ivory portal
    Like music his soft speech must flow! –
If he speak, smile, or walk like a mortal,
    My own Araminta, say 'No!'

Don't listen to tales of his bounty,
    Don't hear what they say of his birth,
Don't look at his seat in the county,
    Don't calculate what he is worth;
But give him a theme to write verse on,
    And see if he turns out his toe;
If he's only an excellent person, –
    My own Araminta, say 'No!'

THE POSIE

O luve will venture in
  Where it daurna weel be seen;
O luve will venture in
  Where wisdom ance has been.
But I will down yon river rove,
  Among the wood sae green –
And a' to pu' a posie
  To my ain dear May.

The primrose I will pu',
  The firstling o' the year,
And I will pu' the pink,
  The emblem o' my dear,
For she's the pink o' womankind,
  And blooms without a peer –
And a' to be a posie
  To my ain dear May.

I'll pu' the budding rose,
  When Phœbus peeps in view,
For it's like a baumy kiss
  O' her sweet bonnie mou';
The hyacinth's for constancy,
  Wi' its unchanging blue –
And a' to be a posie
  To my ain dear May.

The lily it is pure,
  And the lily it is fair,
And in her lovely bosom
  I'll place the lily there;
The daisy's for simplicity,
  And unaffected air —
And a' to be a posie
  To my ain dear May.

The hawthorn I will pu'
  Wi' its locks o' siller gray,
Where, like an aged man,
  It stands at break of day.
But the songster's nest within the bush
  I winna tak away —
And a' to be a posie
  To my ain dear May.

The woodbine I will pu'
  When the e'ening star is near,
And the diamond drops o' dew
  Shall be her e'en sae clear;
The violet's for modesty,
  Which weel she fa's to wear,
And a' to be a posie
  To my ain dear May.

I'll tie the posie round,
  Wi' the silken band o' luve,

And I'll place it in her breast,
   And I'll swear by a' above,
That to my latest draught of life
   The band shall ne'er remove,
And this will be a posie
   To my ain dear May.

ROBERT BURNS (1759–96)

From *SONNETS FROM THE PORTUGUESE*

Belovèd, thou hast brought me many flowers
Plucked in the garden, all the Summer through
And Winter, and it seemed as if they grew
In their close room, nor missed the sun and showers.
So, in the like name of that love of ours,
Take back these thoughts which here unfolded too,
And which on warm and cold days I withdrew
From my heart's ground. Indeed, those beds and
    bowers
Be overgrown with bitter weeds and rue,
And wait thy weeding; yet here's eglantine,
Here's ivy! – take them, as I used to do
Thy flowers, and keep them where they shall not pine.
Instruct thine eyes to keep their colours true,
And tell thy soul, their roots are left in mine.

ELIZABETH BARRETT BROWNING (1806–61)

A DIALOGUE

She. The dandelions in the grass
   Are blown to fairies' clocks;
  On this green bank I pluckt (Alas)
   The last of lady-smocks.
He.   Let them die,
   What care I?
  Roses come when field flowers pass.

She. But these sun-sated sultry hours
   Will make your roses fall:
  Their large wide-open crimson flowers
   Must die like daisies small.
He.   Sweet as yet!
   I'll forget
  (When they die) they lived at all!

A. MARY F. ROBINSON (1857–1944)

'A ROSE HAS THORNS AS WELL AS HONEY'

A rose has thorns as well as honey,
I'll not have her for love or money;
An iris grows so straight and fine,
That she shall be no friend of mine;

Snowdrops like the snow would chill me;
Nightshade would caress and kill me;
Crocus like a spear would fright me;
Dragon's-mouth might bark or bite me;
Convolvulus but blooms to die;
A wind-flower suggests a sigh;
Love-lies-bleeding makes me sad;
And poppy-juice would drive me mad: –
But give me holly, bold and jolly,
Honest, prickly, shining holly;
Pluck me holly leaf and berry
For the day when I make merry.

CHRISTINA ROSSETTI (1830–94)

THE FLOWERS

From golden showers of the ancient skies,
On the first day, and the eternal snow of stars,
You once unfastened giant calyxes
For the young earth still innocent of scars:

Young gladioli with the necks of swans,
Laurels divine, of exiled souls the dream,
Vermilion as the modesty of dawns
Trod by the footsteps of the seraphim;

The hyacinth, the myrtle gleaming bright,
And, like the flesh of woman, the cruel rose,
Hérodiade blooming in the garden light,
She that from wild and radiant blood arose!

And made the sobbing whiteness of the lily
That skims a sea of sighs, and as it wends
Through the blue incense of horizons, palely
Toward the weeping moon in dreams ascends!

Hosanna on the lute and in the censers,
Lady, and of our purgatorial groves!
Through heavenly evenings let the echoes answer,
Sparkling haloes, glances of rapturous love!

Mother, who in your strong and righteous bosom,
Formed calyxes balancing the future flask,
Capacious flowers with the deadly balsam
For the weary poet withering on the husk.

STÉPHANE MALLARMÉ (1842–98)
TR. HENRY WEINFIELD

THE SEND-OFF

Down the close, darkening lanes they sang their way
To the siding-shed,
And lined the train with faces grimly gay.

Their breasts were stuck all white with wreath and
    spray
As men's are, dead.

Dull porters watched them, and a casual tramp
Stood staring hard,
Sorry to miss them from the upland camp.
Then, unmoved, signals nodded, and a lamp
Winked to the guard.

So secretly, like wrongs hushed-up, they went.
They were not ours:
We never heard to which front these were sent.

Nor there if they yet mock what women meant
Who gave them flowers.

Shall they return to beatings of great bells
In wild trainloads?
A few, a few, too few for drums and yells,
May creep back, silent, to still village wells
Up half-known roads.

WILFRED OWEN (1893–1918)   237

CONSIDER THE LILIES OF THE FIELD

Flowers preach to us if we will hear: –
The rose saith in the dewy morn:
I am most fair;
Yet all my loveliness is born
Upon a thorn.
The poppy saith amid the corn:
Let but my scarlet head appear
And I am held in scorn;
Yet juice of subtle virtue lies
Within my cup of curious dyes.
The lilies say: Behold how we
Preach without words of purity.
The violets whisper from the shade
Which their own leaves have made:
Men scent our fragrance on the air,
Yet take no heed
Of humble lessons we would read.

But not alone the fairest flowers:
The merest grass
Along the roadside where we pass,
Lichen and moss and sturdy weed,
Tell of His love who sends the dew,
The rain and sunshine too,
To nourish one small seed.

THE QUESTION

I dream'd that, as I wander'd by the way,
   Bare Winter suddenly was changed to Spring;
And gentle odours led my steps astray,
   Mix'd with a sound of waters murmuring
Along a shelving bank of turf, which lay
   Under a copse, and hardly dared to fling
Its green arms round the bosom of the stream,
But kiss'd it and then fled, as thou mightest in dream.

There grew pied wind-flowers and violets;
   Daisies, those pearl'd Arcturi of the earth,
The constellated flower that never sets;
   Faint oxlips; tender bluebells, at whose birth
The sod scarce heaved; and that tall flower that wets –
   Like a child, half in tenderness and mirth –
Its mother's face with heaven-collected tears
When the low wind, its playmate's voice, it hears.

And in the warm hedge grew lush eglantine,
   Green cowbind and the moonlight-colour'd May,
And cherry-blossoms, and white cups whose wine
   Was the bright dew yet drain'd not by the day;
And wild roses, and ivy serpentine,
   With its dark buds and leaves wandering astray;
And flowers, azure, black, and streak'd with gold,
Fairer than any waken'd eyes behold.

And nearer to the river's trembling edge
   There grew broad flag-flowers, purple prank'd
     with white,
And starry river-buds among the sedge,
   And floating water-lilies, broad and bright,
Which lit the oak that overhung the hedge
   With moonlight beams of their own watery light;
And bulrushes, and reeds of such deep green
As soothed the dazzled eye with sober sheen.

Methought that of these visionary flowers
   I made a nosegay, bound in such a way
That the same hues which in their natural bowers
   Were mingled or opposed, the like array
Kept these imprison'd children of the Hours
   Within my hand; – and then, elate and gay,
I hasten'd to the spot whence I had come,
That I might there present it – O! to whom?

RED TULIPS, THEN ASPHODEL

Was I ever truly happy, like some girl in a red tank top
eating sunlight in Spring?

Hard to say. If flowers are symbols of emotions,
it's still hard to say.

What belongs, what goes, and which way. Did I once
feel like a tulip

bending gracefully toward its own root, its own death,
the lower my head

the more beautiful? Or was I ever showy like a peony
for one wild week,

sexed fully pink without blushing. What are emotions
anyway? Flowers die

not knowing. And yet our feelings lead us down that one
path we only ever take

deceptively edged with bloom after bloom after bloom.

MORAL
From *The Day-Dream*

So, Lady Flora, take my lay,
*   And if you find no moral there,*
Go, look in any glass and say,
*   What moral is in being fair.*
Oh, to what uses shall we put
*   The wildweed-flower that simply blows?*
And is there any moral shut
*   Within the bosom of the rose?*

But any man that walks the mead,
*   In bud or blade, or bloom, may find,*
According to his humours lead,
*   A meaning suited to his mind.*
And liberal applications lie
*   In Art like Nature, dearest friend;*
So 'twere to cramp its use, if I
*   Should hook it to some useful end.*

SELECT GLOSSARY

Victorian language-of-flower vocabularies varied considerably.
The meanings here are largely taken from *The Language and
Poetry of Flowers* (anon., London, 1871); alternative meanings
(which may conflict) are derived from several 19th-century
sources. Other cultural, religious or folk associations are
selectively given, as are symbolic meanings in Eastern cultures.

ALLIUM unity, patience, humility

ANEMONE (WINDFLOWER) sickness, fragility; forsaken love, death
and transience of life (myth of Adonis); red cheeks of the beloved
(Persian/Arabic)

ASPHODEL 'my regret will follow you to the grave'

ASTER/MICHAELMAS DAISY/STARWORT cheerfulness in old age,
farewell; love divination, herb of Venus, formed of stardust
(tears of goddess Astraea)

AZALEA temperance, devoted love, fragile passion; feminine beauty
(Far East)

BLACKTHORN difficulty

BLUEBELL constancy, kindness

BUTTERCUP riches, ingratitude, childishness; sarcasm

  PERSIAN BUTTERCUP (*RANUNCULUS ASIATICA*) radiance, charm

CAMELLIA 'beauty is your only attraction'; perfect loveliness, beauty
and transience; the divine, sudden death (Japan)

CANTERBURY BELL gratitude, constancy

CARNATION strong and pure love; flower of God (*dianthus*), Virgin
Mary's tears

  PINK CARNATION maternal love, woman's love (*see also* PINK)

  RED CARNATION admiration; love, marriage, women's sexuality

  WHITE CARNATION young girl; purity, bad luck, funeral flowers
(Europe and South America)

CELANDINE reawakening, future joy; imparting sight

CHAMOMILE energy in adversity; teeth of the beloved (Persian/ Arabic)

CHERRY BLOSSOM spiritual beauty

CHRYSANTHEMUM cheerfulness in adversity; autumnal rights of the dead (Catholic Europe); longevity, fertility, nobility, integrity, happiness (Far East)

CLOVER (PURPLE) provident, industry

COLCHICUM (AUTUMN CROCUS) 'my best days are past'; bad character

COLUMBINE folly; flower of Venus, sensuality

CONVOLVULUS tender affection, extinguished hopes

COWBIND (WHITE BRYONY) prosperity

COWSLIP pensiveness, attractive grace; keys of heaven

CROCUS cheerfulness; spring and resurrection

CYCLAMEN diffidence; conception, fertility, protection, happiness, sacred to Hecate

DAFFODIL (Narcissus family) deceitful hope, regard, chivalry; Easter associations (wild daffodil = 'Lent lily')

DAHLIA dignity, instability, 'forever thine'; sterile abundance

DAISY innocence, beauty; fidelity, love divination

DANDELION oracle; seduction

DAY-LILY coquetry

EGLANTINE (SWEET BRIER) poetry

EVENING PRIMROSE mildness, silent love, inconstancy

FORGET-ME-NOT true love, faithful remembrance

FOXGLOVE youth, insincerity; magical associations (folk's/fairies' gloves); adulation, flower of Venus, sexual love, fertility

GENTIANS (ALPINE) virgin pride, integrity

FRINGED GENTIAN intrinsic worth, 'I look to heaven'

GERANIUM stupidity and folly, comforting, preference; virtue and morality, respectability

SCARLET GERANIUM moral danger, sexuality

GILLYFLOWER bonds of affection, lasting beauty (*see also* CARNATION, PINK; WALLFLOWER)

HAREBELL 'delicate and lonely as this flower'; submission, grief

HAWTHORN (MAY) hope; marriage, sickness and death

HEARTSEASE *see* PANSY

HEATHER solitude

HIBISCUS delicate beauty; attracting love and lust

HOLLY foresight; king of winter, protection, growth, fertility

HONEYSUCKLE bond of love, sweetness of disposition

    WILD HONEYSUCKLE inconstancy in love; steadfastness in love; wealth, opens eyes to true worth

HYACINTH play or games (myth of Hyacinthus); mourning, hope

    BLUE HYACINTH constancy

    PURPLE HYACINTH sorrow

IRIS message; messenger of the Greek gods whose emblem was the rainbow, royal power and authority

IVY fidelity; friendship, poet's crown, queen of winter, repels negativity and bad luck

JAPONICA (*PYRUS JAPONICA*) excellence

JASMINE (*JESSAMINE*) amiability, grace, simplicity, constancy; divine hope, heavenly felicity; sacred flower used in garlands and ceremonies, marriage and courtship, feminine purity (India); wet season/patient waiting and happiness after marriage (classical Tamil)

JONQUIL (Narcissus family) desire

LARKSPUR levity, fickleness; open heart

LAUREL glory, triumph

LAVENDER, MINT, SAVORY, MARJORAM cures for melancholy

LILY majesty, purity; sovereignty of kings, bridal state, sublime love, procreation, glory, flower of Venus, fertility

LILY, WHITE purity, modesty; virginal innocence, death of young innocents, Virgin Mary, purity of soul, chastity

LILY OF THE VALLEY return of happiness; purity of the Virgin, humility; Celtic good luck charm

LOTUS sacred in Hinduism (creation, birth, female beauty, fecundity, long life, prosperity) and Buddhism (perfection, enlightenment, purity, fruitfulness, creative power); love, erotic love (China)

LOVE-IN-A-MIST perplexity

LOVE-LIES-BLEEDING 'hopeless not heartless'

LUPIN voraciousness, imagination

MARGUERITE/OX-EYE DAISY a token; mouth of the beloved (Persian/Arabic)

MARIGOLD grief, despair, anxiety, jealousy; association with legends of sun-loving Clytie and Caltha; Mary's gold, sorrows of the Virgin; energy, beauty, affection, auspiciousness, sacred flower used in garlands and ceremonies, weddings and funerals (India)

MARYBUD either marsh marigold (kingcup) or calendula (pot marigold) *see* MARIGOLD

MICHAELMAS DAISY *see* ASTER

MIGNONETTE 'your qualities surpass your charms'

MIMOSA (SENSITIVE PLANT) sensitiveness, modesty

MOCK ORANGE (*PHILADELPHUS*) counterfeit

MYRTLE love, marital fidelity; flower of Venus, erotic love, seduction

NARCISSUS self-love (myth of Narcissus); good fortune, happiness (Far East); eyes of the beloved (Persian/Arabic)

OLEANDER (ALSO RHODODENDRON) beware!, danger

ORCHID a belle; exotic beauty, fertility (from Greek *orkhis* – testicle), lust, virility, female sexuality, artificiality, wealth; serenity, nobility, refinement, friendship, virtue, integrity (China and Japan)

PANSY/HEARTSEASE (FIELD PANSY, JOHNNY JUMP UP) thoughts, 'you occupy my thoughts'; love, potency in love charms

PEONY shame, bashfulness; prosperity, reputation, masculinity, feminine beauty, love, spring (Far East)

PIMPERNEL, SCARLET assignation; timekeeper (known as poor man's weatherglass, closing around 2pm or when cloudy)

PINK, GARDEN childishness; betrothal, love and marriage, *see also*
    PINK CARNATION
  STRIPED PINK refusal
POINSETTIA Mexican Christmas flower, fertility, eternity
POPPY (RED) consolation, sleep; oblivion, death, remembrance
  CALIFORNIA POPPY wealth, success
PRIMROSE youth, early days
QUEEN-ANN'S-LACE delicate femininity, sanctuary, fantasy
RAGWORT harvest festival (Celtic), protection against enchantment
ROSE love, beauty, genteel, pretty
ROSE, RED ardent love, courtship, beauty and transience, flower of
    Venus (sexual love, seduction, adulterous love), mortality;
    martyrdom, blood of Christ; perfection and beauty (spiritual or
    worldly), the beloved, manifestation of God's glory, sprung from
    the sweat of the Prophet (Persian/Arabic)
ROSE, WHITE innocence, silence, 'I am worthy of you'; Virgin Mary
    (white rose of Nativity), purity, peace
ROSE, YELLOW infidelity, decrease of love on better acquaintance
ROSEMARY fidelity, remembrance; flower of dead, resurrection
RUE grace, purification; regret, repentance
SNOWDROP consolation, hope, friendship in adversity; purity,
    humility, Mary's sorrow, death
SOLOMON'S SEAL secret; wisdom, protection
SOPPS IN WINE a red clove gillyflower
STAR OF BETHLEHEM comfort, reconciliation, dispels illusions
STOCK lasting beauty
STRAWBERRY FLOWER perfect goodness
SUNFLOWER false riches, pride, pure and lofty thoughts (tall), your
    devoted adorer (short); a Christian's love of God, fidelity and
    constancy, association with myth of Clytie; good luck, long life,
    happiness (China)
SWEET PEA delicate pleasure
SWEET WILLIAM craftiness, sensitivity
THRIFT sympathy; protects against poverty

TULIP declaration of love; beauty and grace; undying or hopeless
    love, perfect beauty, cheek of the beloved, unity of Allah
    (Ottoman/Persian)
VIOLET modesty; Christian humility (Virgin Mary), innocence,
    faithful love
WALLFLOWER fidelity in misfortune
WATER LILY eloquence
  WHITE WATER LILY purity of heart
WOODBINE *see* HONEYSUCKLE

NOTES

1 The name 'Gillyflower' (see note 6) was also applied to fragrant
plants of the mustard family including stock and wallflower. A
legend originating in Scotland told of a maiden imprisoned in a
castle who threw a wallflower plucked from the battlements to her
minstrel lover waiting below before attempting to climb down a
rope to join him. She fell to her death. Medieval troubadours
adopted the wallflower as a symbol of fidelity to a lost love.
2 Elizabeth Barrett to Robert Browning: 'The first you ever gave me
was a yellow rose sent in a letter ... "Infidelity," says the dictionary
of flowers ...!' Browning hastily 'planted a full dozen more rose-
trees, all white – to take away the yellow-rose reproach!' (1846)
3 night violet ('fialka nochnaya'): poetic name for the lesser butterfly
orchid.
4 Probably not the vine but the flowering shrub *azalea viscosa* or
swamp honeysuckle.
5 Xenophon was leading home to Greece his 'Ten Thousand', an
army of mercenaries who had joined the rebellion of Prince Cyrus of
Persia. After an arduous journey they had reached the Pontic moun-
tains lining the Black Sea coast of Anatolia, where highly toxic
rhododendrons and oleanders flourish, now as then. The results of
his soldiers eating 'mad' honey made from the nectar of these

flowers are described by Xenophon in his *Anabasis*. (Nearly five centuries later, the Roman general Pompey did not have such a lucky escape. The locals tempted his soldiers with wild honeycombs and slaughtered them before they could recover from the effects.)

6 Gillyflower (from medieval French *clou de girofle*, a clove, because of their strong scent; or possibly 'July flowers') here refers to striped pinks, carnations or sweet williams. The streaks of colour were associated with loose women.

7 Early editors gave away the (probable) answer to the riddle by entitling this poem 'Purple Clover'.

8 Other flowers have been given the same name, but this Star of Bethlehem is *Catharansus roseus* – the Madagascar periwinkle.

9 Confusingly, this blue bell is Jon Silkin's harebell (*Campanula rotundifolia*) and not at all like Charles Tomlinson's bluebell (*Hyacinthoides non-scripta*).

ACKNOWLEDGMENTS

Thanks are due to the following copyright holders for permission to reprint:

GUILLAUME APOLLINAIRE: 'Autumn Crocuses' from *Effort at Speech: New and Selected Poems of William Meredith*, Northwestern University Press, 1997. AUSONIUS: 'On Newblown Roses', tr. Helen Waddell, from *Medieval Latin Lyrics* by Helen Waddell, Constable, 1929. BASHO: Two narcissus haiku, tr. David Landis Barnhill, from *Basho's Haiku: Selected Poems of Matsuo Basho*, New York State University Press, 2004. IBN BILLITA: 'Marguerite' from *Moorish Poetry* (a translation of *The Pennants*, an anthology compiled in 1243 by the Andalusian Ibn Sa'id), tr. A. J. Arberry, Cambridge University Press, 1953. JORGE LUIS BORGES: 'A Rose and Milton', tr. Alasdair Reid, from *Selected Poems 1923–1967*, ed. Norman Thomas di Giovanni, Allen Lane, 1972. BASIL BUNTING: 'Three Michaelmas Daisies' from *The*

Poems of Basil Bunting, Faber & Faber, 2016. YOSA BUSON: Reprinted with permission from *Japanese Haiku*, translated by Peter Beilenson and originally published in 1955 by Peter Pauper Press, Inc., White Plains, New York, USA. www.peterpauper.com. CHANG YU: 'Yellow Sunflower of Szechwan', tr. Irving Y. Lo, from *Sunflower Splendor: Three Thousand Years of Chinese Poetry*, ed. Wu-chi Liu and Irving Yucheng Lo, Anchor Books, Doubleday, 1975. AMY CLAMPITT: 'The Smaller Orchid' and 'The Field Pansy' from *The Collected Poems of Amy Clampitt*. Alfred A. Knopf, 1997. Faber & Faber, 1998. IBN DARRAJ AL-QASTALLI: 'Lilies', tr. Cola Franzen, from *Poems of Arab Andalusia*. Copyright © 1989 Cola Franzen. Reprinted with the permission of The Permissions Company, Inc., on behalf of City Lights Books, www.citylights.com. ROSALÍA DE CASTRO: 'In My Small Garden' from *Rosalía de Castro: Poems*, ed. and tr. Anna-Maria Aldaz, Barbara N. Gantt and Anne C. Bromley, State University of New York Press, 1991. SOR JUANA INÉS DE LA CRUZ: Sonnet 147: 'In which she morally censures a rose, and thereby all that resemble it' from *Sor Juana Inés de la Cruz: Selected Works*, tr. Edith Grossman, ed. Anna Moore, Norton Critical Editions, 2016. WALTER DE LA MARE: 'The Hawthorn Hath a Deathly Smell' and 'Noon and Night Flower' from *The Listeners*, 1912. With permission from The Literary Trustees of Walter de la Mare and The Society of Authors as their representative. LORENZO DE' MEDICI: Sonnet XCIV: 'O Lovely Violet' from *The Complete Literary Works of Lorenzo de' Medici*, ed. and tr. Guido A. Guarino. New York: Italica Press, 2016. Copyright 2016 by Italica Press. Used by permission of Italica Press. EMILY DICKINSON: 'So has a daisy vanished' and 'I was the slightest in the house' from *Bolts of Melody: New Poems of Emily Dickinson*, ed. Mabel Loomis Todd and Millicent Todd Bingham, Harvard University Press, 1945. 'Through the Dark Sod' from *The Poems of Emily Dickinson, the Definitive Edition*, ed. Martha Dickinson Bianchi and Alfred Leete Hampson (first published in 1929 in *Further Poems*), Harvard University Press, 1933. HD (HILDA DOOLITTLE): 'Sea Rose' from *The Sea Garden*, 1916. 'Leda' from *Hymen*, New Directions,

1921. CAROL ANN DUFFY: 'Demeter' from *Collected Poems*, Picador, 2015. JOHN EPPEL: 'Star of Bethlehem' from *Songs My Country Taught Me: Selected Poems 1965–2005*, Weaver Press, 2005. U. A. FANTHORPE: 'Daffodil Ministry' from *Collected Poems 1978–2003*, Peterloo Poets, 2005. Reprinted with permission from Dr R. V. Bailey. JAMES FENTON: 'Yellow Tulips' from *Selected Poems*, Penguin, 2006. VICKI FEAVER: 'Marigolds' from *The Handless Maiden*, Jonathan Cape, 1994. THÉOPHILE GAUTIER: 'The Tea-Rose' from *Selected Lyrics: Théophile Gautier*, tr. Norman R. Shapiro, Margellos World Republic of Letters, Yale University Press, 2010. Reprinted with permission. LOUISE GLÜCK: 'Mock Orange' from *The First Four Books of Poems*, Ecco Press/HarperCollins, 1995. 'The Silver Lily' from *The Wild Iris*, Ecco Press/HarperCollins, 1992. J. W. VON GOETHE: 'Rosebud in the Heather', tr. John Frederick Nims, in Goethe: *Selected Works*, Everyman's Library, taken from *Sappho to Valéry*, copyright © 1971 by John Frederick Nims. Princeton University Press. HAFEZ: 'The Nightingale and the Rose', tr. A. J. Arberry, from *Fifty Poems of Hafiz*, Cambridge University Press, 1962. SEAMUS HEANEY: 'Lupins' from *New Selected Poems 1988–2013*, Faber & Faber, 2014. ANTHONY HECHT: 'Look Deep' from *The Darkness and the Light: Poems* by Anthony Hecht, copyright © 2001 by Anthony E. Hecht. Used by permission of Alfred A. Knopf, an imprint of the Knopf Doubleday Publishing Group, a division of Penguin Random House LLC. All rights reserved. Any third party use of this material, outside of this publication, is prohibited. Interested parties must apply directly to Penguin Random House LLC for permission. Waywiser Press, London, 2002. HEINRICH HEINE: 'Lotus Blossom' from Heinrich Heine, *Songs of Love and Grief: A Bilingual Anthology*, tr. Walter W. Arndt, Northwestern University Press, 1995. HUANG E: 'To the Tune of "Soaring"' tr. Kenneth Rexroth, from *The Orchid Boat: Women Poets of China* by Kenneth Rexroth, McGraw Hill, 1972. TED HUGHES: 'Sunstruck Foxglove' from *Flowers and Insects*, Faber & Faber, 1986. 'Snowdrop' from *Collected Poems* (ed. Paul Keegan), Faber & Faber, 2003. VICTOR HUGO: 'My Two Daughters', tr. Peter

Dale Scott. ISSA: Haiku: irises (irises), Haiku: the little shrine (azaleas), and Haiku: winter wind (camellia), tr. David G. Lanoue, (www.haikuguy.com/issa). Reprinted with the kind permission of the translator. KAO CH'I: 'Sunflower', tr. Irving Y. Lo, from *Sunflower Splendor: Three Thousand Years of Chinese Poetry*, ed. Wu-chi Liu and Irving Yucheng Lo, Anchor Books, Doubleday, 1975. MIMI KHALVATI: 'Ghazal: Lillies of the Valley' from *The Meanest Flower*, Carcanet Press, 2007. D. H. LAWRENCE: 'Bavarian Gentians' from *Last Poems*, Viking/Penguin, 1932; 'Sicilian Cyclamens' from *Birds Beasts and Flowers*, Viking/Penguin, 1923. DENISE LEVERTOV: 'In Praise of Allium' from *Breathing the Water*, New Directions, 1987, Bloodaxe Books, 1988. Reprinted with permission. STÉPHANE MALLARMÉ: 'The Flowers' from *Collected Poems: A Bilingual Edition*, tr. Henry Weinfeld, University of California Press, 1994. ROY MARSHALL: 'Dandytime' from *The Sun Bathers*. Copyright © 2013 by Roy Marshall. Reprinted with permission from the poet and Shoestring Press. JOSÉ MARTÍ: Poem xxxix (A White Rose), tr. Manuel A. Tellemachea, from *Martí's Versos Sencillos: Simple Verses*, Arte Publico Press, University of Houston, 1997. MEDBH MCGUCKIAN: 'The Orchid House' from *The Flower Master and Other Poems*, Oxford University Press, 1982. EUGENIO MONTALE: 'The Sunflower, tr. Patricia Hann. MARIANNE MOORE: 'Injudicious Gardening' and 'Rosemary' from *Marianne Moore: Observations*, Farrar, Straus & Giroux, 2016. Faber & Faber. ABDALLAH IBN AL-MU'TAZZ: 'Looking, the narcissus, looking', tr. Andras Hamori, from *Literature East and West 15* (1971), pp. 495–7, Luzac & Co, London. SAROJINI NAIDU: 'The Lotus' from *The Broken Wing: Songs of Love, Death and Destiny 1915–1916*. John Lane, New York, Heinemann, London. KIRIN NARAYAN: 'Kangra Folk Song' (anon.) taken from *Singing Goddesses in the Himalayan Foothills* by Kirin Narayan, University of Chicago Press, 2016. NECATI: 'Gazel', tr. John R. Walsh, from *The Penguin Book of Turkish Verse*, ed. Nermin Menemencioglu and Fahir Iz, 1978. MARY OLIVER: 'Poppies' from *New and Selected Poems*, Beacon Press, 1992. ALICE OSWALD: 'Violet' and 'Thrift' from *Weeds and Wild Flowers, Poems by Alice*

253

Editorial Publications, Inc; from *Collected Poems* by Theodore
Roethke. Used by permission of Doubleday, an imprint of the Knopf
Doubleday Publishing Group, a division of Penguin Random House
LLC. All rights reserved. Faber & Faber. RUMI: 'The Rose' from
Fundamentals of Rumi's Thought: A Mevlevi-Sufi Perspective by Sefik
Can, tr. Zeki Saritoprak, The Light, Inc, 2005. RYOKAN: 'The Lotus'
and 'I descended to the valley to gather orchids' from *Dewdrops on a
Lotus Leaf: Zen Poems* by Ryokan, tr. John Stevens, Shambhala,
2004. RYOTA: Haiku (chrysanthemum) from *Haiku, vol. 4*, translated
by R. H. Blyth, The Hokuseido Press, 1952. IBN SA'ID: 'The Virgin'
from *Moorish Poetry* (a translation of *The Pennants,* an anthology
compiled in 1243 by the Andalusian Ibn Sa'id), tr. A. J. Arberry,
Cambridge University Press, 1953. al-Sanawbari: 'Eyes of Narcissi',
tr. Michelle Quay, used with permission of the translator. SAPPHO:
'... frankly I wish I were dead', tr. Josephine Balmer, from *Sappho,
Poems & Fragments,* tr. Josephine Balmer, Bloodaxe Books, 1992.
Reprinted with permission from Bloodaxe Books. E. J. SCOVELL:
'Deaths of Flowers' from *Selected Poems,* Carcanet Press, 1991. 'Mid-
Winter Flowers' (excerpt) from *Collected Poems,* Carcanet Press,
1988. BRENDA SHAUGHNESSY: 'Red Tulips, Then Asphodel' from *So
Much Synth,* Copper Canyon Press, 2016. JON SILKIN: 'A Daisy' and
'Harebell' from *Jon Silkin: Complete Poems,* ed. Jon Glover and
Kathryn Jenner, Carcanet Press, 2015. KIM SOWŏL: 'Azaleas', tr.
David R. McCann, from *Modern Korean Literature: An Anthology,* ed.
Peter H. Lee, University Press of Hawaii, 1990. ANNE STEVENSON:
'Ragwort' from *Anne Stevenson: The Collected Poems 1955–1995,*
Oxford University Press, 1996. RABINDRANATH TAGORE: 'The First
Jasmines' from *Collected Poems and Plays of Rabandranath Tagore,*
1936, Macmillan. CHARLES TOMLINSON: 'The Metamorphosis' and
'The Order of Saying' from *New and Collected Poems,* Carcanet Press,
2009. VAYILANREVAN: 'What She Said' (Kuruntokai 108), from *Poems
of Love and War,* tr. and ed. A. K. Ramanujan, Columbia University
Press, 1985. PAUL VERLAINE: 'A Dahlia' from *One Hundred and One
Poems of Paul Verlaine: A Bilingual Edition,* tr. Norman R. Shapiro,

University of Chicago Press, 1998. WANG WEI: 'Red Peonies', tr. Irving Y. Lo, from *Sunflower Splendor: Three Thousand Years of Chinese Poetry*, ed. Wu-chi Liu and Irving Yucheng Lo, Anchor Books, Doubleday, 1975. SALLY WEN MAO: 'Mad Honey Soliloquy' from *Mad Honey Symposium*, Alice James Books, 2014. RICHARD WILBUR: 'Signatures' from *Collected Poems 1943–2004*, Harcourt Inc. Copyright © 2004 by Richard Wilbur. Published 2005 in UK by Waywiser Press by arrangement with Harcourt. WILLIAM CARLOS WILLIAMS: 'Iris' and 'Queen-Ann's-Lace' from *Collected Poems of William Carlos Williams, vol. 2 (1939–1962)*, New Directions. EMPEROR WU-TI: 'The Autumn Wind' from *One Hundred and Seventy Chinese Poems*, tr. Arthur Waley. The Estate of Arthur Waley. EMPEROR YANG: 'Peonies at Jinxing Temple', tr. anon., found in *Roses and Peonies: Flower Poetics in Western and Eastern Translation*, 2014. Ibn al-Zaqqaq: 'Anemones', tr. Arie Schippers, from *Spanish Hebrew Poetry and the Arabic Tradition: Arabic Themes in Hebrew Andalusian Poetry* by Arie Schippers, E. J. Brill, 1994. Reprinted with permission.